BIBLICA ET ORIENTALIA

(SACRA SCRIPTURA ANTIQUITATIBUS ORIENTALIBUS ILLUSTRATA)

11a

ROMAE
E PONTIFICIO INSTITUTO BIBLICO
1984

THOMAS J. O'SHAUGHNESSY, S.J.
San Jose Major Seminary, Manila

Word of God in the Qur'ān

Second, completely revised edition of
The Koranic Concept of the Word of God

ROME
BIBLICAL INSTITUTE PRESS
1984

This is a completely revised edition of
The Koranic Concept of the Word of God (Biblica et Orientalia, 11)
by Thomas O'Shaughnessy, S.J.
(Roma: Pontificio Istituto Biblico, 1948)

ISBN 88-7653-340-0

PRINTED IN ITALY

TYPIS PONTIFICIAE UNIVERSITATIS GREGORIANAE — ROMAE

Foreword

The present investigation into the meaning of word of God in the Qur'ān is a revision of a study first published in 1948. This recasting tries to keep and update anything of value in the previous work and to eliminate its imperfections. It recognizes the religious value of the essential parts of the Qur'ānic message—monotheism, prophethood, adoration due to the one true God, and faith in his word.

Prophetic missions advocating truths found also in Christ's teaching can arise outside the Church (Nostra Aetate, 2-3). Vatican Council II sees in the religious endeavors by which adherents of world religions search for God part of his universal design for the salvation of the human race (Ad Gentes, 3). If this is true of world religions in general, it is even more valid for Islam, which arose in surroundings already influenced for centuries by Judaism and Christianity.

Even as regards the topic dealt with here the Qur'ān does not set itself in opposition to any Biblical teaching. Christian belief in Jesus as Word is based on his procession from the first Person of the Trinity as that Person's perfect expression. But Christians also hold that the eternal Word became incarnate in the Virgin Mary by a special action of God in her which can be seen as a creative intervention. It is because of this creative intervention that the Qur'ān, as this study will attempt to show, would give the title "word" to Jesus.

But an investigation of this kind has other advantages. The Qur'ānic use of terms found also in Christianity is a partial concretizing of some of the theological disputes that disturbed the Church of the early centuries. This is especially true in regard to the key notion, "word of God," given as a title to Jesus in several places in the Qur'ān. But inquiry into its meaning should aim at discovering what the Qur'ān wishes its hearers to understand by the term. It should not seek to point out inconsistencies based on the assumption that it intends to use "word of God" in its Christian sense. In this matter as in most others a polemic approach cannot contribute to objectivity and mutual understanding. These goals will be better met by finding common grounds with Islam where this is possible and by seeing in them part of the Creator's salvific plan for mankind.

The transliteration of Arabic words is that of *The Encyclopaedia of Islam*, new edition (London: Luzac, 1960, continuing) with the following exceptions: (1) q instead of ḳ and j instead of dj; (2) Dhāl, Ghain, Khā, Shīn, and Thā are represented by dh, gh, kh, sh, and th without the ligature; (3) the Lām of the article is assimilated before the so-called solar letters (see W. Wright, *A Grammar of the Arabic Language*, 3rd edition, two volumes (London: Cambridge University Press, 1979), i. 15, C).

Table of Contents

1. The Arabic *kalima* and Its Theological Equivalents

The noun *kalima* (verb: *kallama*, he addressed, he spoke) is the most general term corresponding to "word." Word can mean the external articulate sound that conveys an idea or the internal concept or mental term. Aristotle in *De Interpretatione* sums up the relationship between the two meanings: "Spoken words are the symbols of mental experience and written words are the symbols of spoken words." [1]

In Arabic the radical meaning of the noun is more closely associated with mental experience and coherent phrasing than its English equivalent. Besides its ordinary sense of "word," *kalima* often expresses notions like discourse, opinion, decree or maxim. Some of these meanings are illustrated by the idiomatic expressions, *tashattatat kalimatuhum*, "they disagreed" (literally, "their word was scattered"), *jamaʿa kalimatahum*, "he reconciled them" (literally, "he joined their word"), *ikhtilāfu l-kalima*, "discord" (literally, "a differing of word"), and *anshada kalimatan*, "he recited a poem" (literally, "a word").[2] *Kalima* is therefore the best equivalent of the Scriptural *logos* and the Christian theological term *verbum*. The translators of the Septuagint usually rendered the Hebrew *dābār* by *logos*, which in Arabic versions became *kalima*. This term best signifies the outward form of expression, the utterance, the word, and the inward power of mind manifested in speech. Both these aspects belong to the original meaning of *logos* and to the strictly personal sense it was later to acquire in the New Testament.[3]

The Hebrew noun *dābār* shows a like correspondance of ideas. Its dianoetic sense of thought or meaning is that which makes an object knowable, so that to comprehend the *dābār* of a thing is to comprehend the thing itself. *Dābār* also has a dynamic element. This makes it a synonym of effective power, which is felt by the one who takes the word to himself and is

---

1 *De Interpretatione*, 16 a 1, tr. by E. M. Edghill, *The Works of Aristotle*, ed. by W. D. Ross (London: Oxford University Press, 1950), I.

2 Ṭabarī cites the last mentioned example. Aṭ-Ṭabarī, Abū Jaʿfar Muḥammad ibn Jarīr, *Jāmiʿ al-bayān fī tafsīr al-qur'ān*, edited by Maḥmūd Muḥammad Shākir (16 vols. incomp., Cairo: Dār al-Maʿārif, 1957-68), 6, 374, on 3. 39/34.

3 See Henry G. Liddell and Robert Scott, *A Greek-English Lexicon* (9th ed.; Oxford: The Clarendon Press, 1966), sub vv. *logos*, X, and *lego*, B, II and III, pp. 1059 and 1034.

present independently in the objective effects of the word in history.[4] Words of blessing or cursing in particular, once uttered, have an effectiveness that extends far into the future.[5]

In two texts the parallel sense of *dābār, logos*, and *kalima* has special relevance for the present subject: (1) In Ps 33.6, "By the word of the Lord the heavens were made," *dābār*, designating God's creative command, becomes *logos* in the Septuagint and *kalima* in the Arabic versions; (2) In Ez 37.4-5, "O dry bones, hear the word of the Lord. Thus says the Lord God to these bones: Behold, I will cause breath to enter you, and you shall live." Here *dābār*, God's word of command, portrayed as effecting the resurrection of the dead, is likewise expressed by *logos* and *kalima*.

In a number of other passages throughout the Old Testament word signifies God's decree or his efficacious power.[6] These too use the same Greek and Arabic terms to translate *dābār*. Examples would be Ps 147.15, 18, "He sends forth his command to the earth; his word runs swiftly. ... He sends forth his word and melts them," and Ps 107.20, "He sent forth his word and healed them, and delivered them from destruction." The Old Testament also uses word for divine revelation given to a prophet. In this sense too *logos* and *kalima* are the equivalents of *dābār*: "Now the word of the Lord came to me saying, 'Before I formed you in the womb I knew you,'" and "The word of the Lord that came to Hosea, the son of Beeri."[7]

On the contrary, Scripture uses a different term where it stresses the enunciation or the oracular quality of word. In Nm 24.4, for example, "The oracle of him who hears the words of God," *ēmer* becomes *logion* in the Septuagint and *qawl* in the Arabic version. The same correspondence appears also in Ps 19.14, "Let the words of my mouth ... be acceptable in thy sight, O Lord," "Mere talk," in Hebrew *dābār*, is *logos* in the Septuagint and *kalām* in Arabic in Is 36.5, "Do you think that mere words are strategy and power for war?" and Eccl 10.14, "A fool multiplies words, though no man knows what is to be." "A thing said" is *dābār, rhēma*, and *kalām* in Gn 31.1: "But ... he heard the words of the sons of Laban: Jacob has taken away all," while "utterance" is *imra, rhēma*, and *maqala* in Dt 32.2, "May my speech distil as the dew."

Talmudic and Rabbinic writings exerted notable influence on the religious thought of pre-Islamic Arabia through the many Jewish colonies established there. Hence the relation of *logos* to the Rabbinic *mēmrā'*, "word," deserves to be considered in seeking Jewish counterparts of Islamic

---

[4] Gerhard Kittel, *Theological Dictionary of the New Testament* (10 vols.; Grand Rapids: Eerdmans Publishing Company, 1964-76), 4, 92.

[5] Gen 20.7; Jos 6.26; 1 Kgs 16.34.

[6] Jules Lebreton, *Les origines du dogme de la Trinité* (Paris: Beauchesne, 1927), 6th ed., p. 131.

[7] Jer 1.4f and Hos 1.1. See also Mi 1.1 and Zeph 1.1.

terminology. The *mēmrā'* is one of the many intermediate agents, personal and impersonal, between God and the created universe, which were intended to guard the divine transcendence. In Chaldean and Aramaic paraphrasings of Scripture the word (*mēmrā'*) of Yahweh occurs often in a personified form, but never as an individual entity distinct from God. Yahweh utters the word and the universe comes into being; his *mēmrā'* providentially guards the Chosen People from misfortune, imparts the words of the Law, and moves the prophets to speak in his name. In these poetical personifications the *mēmrā'* is sometimes represented as Yahweh's messenger or as the divine omnipotence. But it appears most often as a simple substitute for the name of God where the Targumist from religious scruple dares not ascribe to God deeds or words which in his opinion are incompatible with the divine attributes. So where Is 66. 13 says, "As one whom his mother comforts, so I will comfort you; you shall be comforted in Jerusalem," the Targumist writes, "So my *mēmrā'* will comfort you." [8]

Some of these uses of *mēmrā'* recall passages in the Qur'ān which use *kalima* as a synonym for the divine decree. So Is 1. 20, "You shall be devoured by the sword; for the mouth of the Lord has spoken," becomes in the paraphrase of the Targumist Jonathan: "You shall be killed by the sword, because so has the word (*mēmrā'*) of the Lord decided it," while the Qur'ān in 42. 21/20 [9] says, "Had it not been for the word (*kalima*) of decision, judgment would have been given" and in 10. 19/20, "People were only one community, then they disagreed; and had it not been for your Lord's decree (*kalima*) already passed, decision would have been given between them." But the similarity in such passages seems to be based on a definite sense given to *kalima* in the Qur'ān, as will be seen presently, whereas in the Targums *mēmrā'* is merely a substitute for the divine decree, God's spoken word or God himself, which here happens to approximate later Qur'ānic usage. Jewish influence on the Qur'ān appears more clearly in the Qur'ānic use of such typically Hebrew terms as *shekēnā* (Arabic *sakīna*) [10] or the symbol of God's presence, identified with *logos* and *mēmrā'* by the authors of the Talmud and made an intermediary between God and the world by the Jewish philosopher Philo. [11]

Like the writers of the Old Testament, and even to a more marked degree, the Jewish-Alexandrian theologians in their use of *logos* traced a path which paralleled that of Messianism but never joined it. This is worth noting not

---

[8] Lebreton, *Les origines*, p. 163.

[9] In the Qur'ānic references where the verse-number in Flügel's edition differs from that in the standard Egyptian edition, that of Flügel is given after a diagonal.

[10] 2. 248/249; 9. 26, 40; 48. 4, 18, 26.

[11] A. Michel, "Jésus Christ—La théologie juive—Le verbe ou logos," *Dictionnaire de Théologie Catholique*, ed. by A. Vacant et al. (18 vols.; Paris: Librairie Letouzey et Ané, 1909-72), 8 (1924), col. 1131.

only because of the influence their speculation may have exercised on the selection of the term used in John's Gospel[12] and thus indirectly on the Qur'ānic use, but also because of their importance to the general religious scene in which Islam had its rise.

Even before Philo, Jewish theology had developed the notion of a *logos* and had assigned it a role somewhat similar to that of Wisdom. But in the Alexandrian world of theological speculation *logos* acquired meanings whose very multiplicity renders impossible any determination of its influence in the Christian centers of south-western Asia.[13] With Philo, however, the term finds its most complete pre-Joannine development. For him the *Logos* was the solution of a philosophical problem. God is transcendent; separating him and his creature, man, is an infinite gulf. Yet between this transcendent being and mankind there exist relations of prayer, revelation and providential guidance. To establish these relationships and to unite man with God Philo postulates a *Logos*, chief of the powers intermediary between God and men, the first of the angels, symbolically identified, in his mind, with the Angel of the Lord of the Old Testament. The imagination must represent this extraordinary being as vast enough to fill the infinite distance between the creature and the Creator and to touch both "at their extremities."

In this last postulate the weakness of the system appears. What kind of intermediary can bridge an infinite distance? If it is God, it is also inaccessible to men; if a creature, God is beyond its reach.[14] Philo tries to evade the difficulty by a verbal solution. The *Logos* is "neither uncreated, like God, nor created, like us." The phrase is a premonition of the dispute that was to disrupt Islam centuries later when applied to the Qur'ān as the uncreated word of God. Philo's solution proposes an entity defined by negations which are mutually destructive. Only in Christ, the personal *Logos*, which Philo fell short of conceiving, can two terms so seemingly incompatible find meaning. He is not intermediate between two natures, but unites divinity and humanity in his Person. Unlike Philo's *Logos*, neither uncreated nor created, Christ is both, as the Word made flesh.

In the New Testament and the Christian ecclesiastical writers *logos-kalima* portrays the divine Person first mentioned in Ap 19.13: "He is clad in a robe dipped in blood, and the name by which he is called is the Word of God." Here the term also bears the principal meanings consecrated by Old Testament usage. Among these various acceptations are three that were later to modify the religious thought of Islam and to occasion disputes among its theologians: divine revelation objectively understood, the creative word, and the Word as a divine Person.

---

[12] Lebreton, *Les origines*, xvi.
[13] Ibid., p. 496.
[14] Ibid., p. 249.

Logos indicating the content of divine revelation occurs often throughout the entire New Testament. Christ imparts to the Apostles the word of the Father.[15] The preachers of the Gospel announce the word of God.[16] Their hearers receive it[17] and are elevated to a new life by the supernatural helps revealed and established by Christ and briefly expressed in the phrase, "the word of God."[18]

The prologue of the Fourth Gospel, by its apparently intentional reference to the account of creation in Genesis, represents the world as created by God's word: "In the beginning was the Word (*logos, kalima*). ... All things were made through him: and without him was not anything made that was made."[19] The same notion recurs in 2 Pt, which speaks of the origin of things by God's creative word: "They deliberately ignore this fact, that by the word (*logos, kalima*) of God heavens existed long ago and an earth formed out of water. ..." The divine creative act sustains the universe by the same all-powerful word: "But by the same word (*logos, kalima*) the heavens and earth that now exist have been ... kept until the day of judgment."[20]

Some ecclesiastical writers, while not denying the immaterial and uncreated nature of God's operation in producing the universe, nevertheless declared that the Creator made use of a perceptible command to manifest his action to the spirits present before Him.[21] Saint Augustine objects to this attempt to liken the word of creation to the audible approval of the Father at Christ's baptism, terming it an absurd and carnal notion. By the voice of God we must understand the content of the expression *Fiat lux* rather than the material sound. Moreover, as "all things were made through the Word,"[22] light also was made by him when God pronounced the command of creation. So, the word *Fiat lux* is eternal, since the Word of God is God and coeternal with the Father, although the creature produced by it is temporal.[23]

Finally, against the Subordinationist theories that had attacked the Son's consubstantiality with the Father, the word of creation is not an order given to

---

[15] Jn 17.14.

[16] Acts 4.29, 31.

[17] Acts 8.14; 13.7.

[18] 1 Pt 1.23.

[19] Jn 1.1, 3.

[20] 2 Pt 3.5, 7. The philological comparisons in this chapter are not an attempt to limit the meanings of word to the examples given, since there is much liberty in Scriptural usage, but rather aim to show by contrast that *kalima* roughly corresponds to the sense already explained.

[21] So Theodoretus Episc. Cyrens., *Quaest. in Genes.*, cap. 1, Interrog. 9; *Patr. Gr.*, 80, col. 90, and Basilius Seleuciensis, *Orationes*, 1, 2; P.G., 85, col. 30-31.

[22] Jn I. 1, 3.

[23] St. Augustine, *The Literal Meaning of Genesis*, tr. by John Hammond Taylor (New York: Newman Press, 1982), I, Book One, ch. 2, nn. 5-6, pp. 21-22.

the second Person, since he himself is the very Word of the Father. Only in this identification with the Son, as the *Verbum mentale* proceeding from the divine intellect, can "word" bear a proper sense when applied to God. In all its other meanings it is predicated of the Deity figuratively and by way of metaphor.[24]

The *Dixitque Deus* of Gn 1.3, then, is God's personal will expressed in his word. This word is not oral but mental, not the product of a reasoning power, which is non-existent in God, but an essential word common to the three divine persons. The thing understood and its expression are, in God, numerically one in nature with the one understanding and expressing. So for God to speak, in this context, is to conceive mentally, to will, decree, and efficaciously to command. By his very conceiving and willing he brings the created object into being. Creation is a work common to the Trinity but the *Dixit* of Gn 1.3 is appropriated to the Son as the word proceeding from the Father through an operation of the divine intellect.

In Christian belief, therefore, as well as in Scripture, Word and Wisdom are the terms used to indicate the manner of the Son's procession from the Father. The Word in this sense is not exteriorly given forth but immanent, remaining within the divine intellect: "The Word was with God;... the only Son, who is in the bosom of the Father."[25] This Word, one in essence with the Father, proceeds from him by an intellectual operation in which he utters it; that is to say, expresses a perfect likeness of himself.[26] Christian usage, then, regards Word as a proper name designating the second Person of the Trinity, for in this term is implied the intellectual procession which is proper to the Son alone.

As will be seen later, Muslim speculation on the word of God takes a direction differing widely from that of Christian theology, even though many of the basic problems—creation, the divine attributes, God's activity in the world—are the same in both systems. Islam regards the word of God, not as a living individual, but as an accident or, at most, an attribute really distinct from the Creator. It is, moreover, conceived of as in potency—utterable before pronounced—and infinitely multiple, concepts which in Christian theology are opposed to God's perfection.

2. Word in the Qur'ān

Kalima occurs in a variety of meanings in the sacred book of Islam. It is found there forty-six times; twenty-seven as a singular noun, *kalima*, fifteen

---

[24] *Summa Theologica*, 1, q. 34, a. 1.

[25] Jn 1.1,18.

[26] See *Summa Theol.*, 1, qq. 27 and 34.

times as a sound plural *kalimāt*, and four as a broken plural.[27] To obtain a general view of its use in the Qur'ān both in its ordinary sense and as a term to indicate a definite religious concept or phenomenon, the various grammatical forms are best treated separately.

The broken plural, *kalim*, in its four occurrences,[28] indicates "words" literally understood; thrice the revealed words of the Old Testament—the Jewish Torah—as the Qur'ān understands it, and once[29] of the words of Islamic worship or the profession of faith in one God, "There is no deity but God," which is described as an act of merit in the sight of the Creator. In the first three passages *kalim* is used as part of a formula: *yuḥarrifūna l-kalima ʿan mawaḍiʿihi* in which the Jews are accused of tampering with the words of Scripture in order to delete any mention of Muhammad's coming.

Kalimāt, the sound plural form, is used in several different senses in its fifteen appearances in the Qur'ān.[30] In nine places it signifies "words of revelation," either in a material sense—words written down with pen and ink[31]—or in the sense of a revealed message imparted to Muhammad.[32] Four times[33] this plural occurs in or in context with a set phrase, *lā mubaddila (tabdīla) likalimati llāh*, "(there is) no changing God's words," where "words" indicates "promises," so that the expression is commonly interpreted, "There is no breaking of God's promises."[34] Finally, *kalimāt* is found twice[35] in the meaning of divine precepts given to Mary, mother of Jesus, and to Abraham, both persons esteemed for their sanctity and regarded in the Qur'ān as models worthy of imitation.

But the term is used most often in its singular form *kalima*; twenty-seven times[36] in all, as has already been said, and in five main acceptations exclusive of its occurrences in the three Christological texts. The most common of

---

[27] See Gustavus Flügel, *Concordantiae Corani Arabice* (ed. stereotypa; Ridgewood: Gregg Press, 1965), *s. vv.*

[28] 4.46/48; 5.13/16, 41/45; 35.10/11.

[29] 35.10/11.

[30] 2.37/35; 7.158; 8.7; 10.82; 18.27/26, 109(*bis*); 31.27/26; and 40.22/23. In 18.27/26 the context and the interpretation of the commentators support the meaning of revelation, though a formula generally accompanying another sense is used.

[31] E.g., 18.109.

[32] 7.158.

[33] I.e., 6.34, 115(*bis*), and 10.64/65.

[34] Ṭabarī, *Jāmiʿ al-bayān* on 10.64/65; vol. 15, 141; and Jalālayn, *Tafsīr* on 10.64/65.

[35] 2.124/118 and 66.12.

[36] 3.39/34, 45/40, 64/57; 4.171/169; 7.137/133; 9.40(*bis*), 74/75; 10.19/20, 33/34, 96; 11.110/112, 119/120; 14.24/29, 26/31; 18.5/4; 20.129; 23.100/102; 37.171; 39.19/20, 71; 40.6; 41.45; 42.14/13, 21/20; 43.28/27; and 48.26.

these acceptations is "divine decree";[37] a decree to grant victory or to bless with bounty,[38] but most frequently the decree predestining to hell and delaying judgment and requital until the Day of Resurrection.

The "word" of predestination to hell is nearly always used in a fixed formula,[39] "*ḥaqqat kalimatu rabbika (kalimatu l-ʿadhābi) ʿalā*": "The word of thy Lord (the word of punishment) has come true against." This "word," pronounced against the evildoers predestined in God's plans to eternal punishment, is the decree enuntiated in 11. 119/120, the first of the passages proclaimed (i.e., in the generally accepted chronological order),[40] where it is found in this exact sense: "The word of thy Lord is fulfilled, 'I will surely fill hell with jinns and men together'." It is interesting to note that this use of "word" occurs only in the chapters attributed to the last three or four years of Muhammad's stay at Mecca. There when the storm of persecution rose high against him, the Qur'ān pictures his foes suffering in the fires of hell.

God's "word" or decree to delay requital until the Day of Resurrection is also part of a formula in its six appearances:[41] *Walawlā kalimatun sabaqat min rabbika*, "And had it not been for thy Lord's word already announced." God's word or decree in the Qur'ān is, indeed, represented as an act of the mind and will but what impresses one most is its arbitrary character. The reader is always left with the impression that God has so decided, but to have decreed the contrary would have been just as much in keeping with his infinite perfection. The Qur'ānic narrative pictures God as the omnipotent master in sending souls to hell. Hell is to be filled because the all powerful Creator has so decided. Altogether absent is the notion of satisfaction required to restore right order that has been disturbed by the wilful malice of a creature.

After the meaning of decree, "word" occurs most commonly in the Qur'ān in the sense of a profession of belief, either the Islamic profession of faith in one God or the unbelievers' profession of polytheism. The term is so used six times[42] and in two places it is found in the meaning in which it has been accepted with its modifier as a technical term in Islamic theology and ritual. "*Kalimatan baqiyatan*" in 43. 28/27, literally "a lasting word," which Abraham is said to have given to his posterity, is now a synonym for the *tawḥīd* or the Muslim profession of faith in God's unicity: "There is no deity but God." In 48. 26, too, the *kalimata t-taqwā* which God requires believers to accept is the full profession of Islamic creed, "There is no deity but God and Muhammad is God's apostle," called "the word of piety," as the Jalālain note in their commentary, because it produces that virtue in the one uttering it.

---

[37] In sūras 7, 10, 11, 20, 37, 39, 40, 41, and 42.
[38] 37. 171; and 7. 137/133.
[39] 10. 33/34, 96; 11. 119/120; 39. 19/20, 71; 40. 6.
[40] According to Nöldeke's chronological arrangement of the sūras.
[41] 10. 19/20; 11. 110/112; 20. 129; 41. 45; 42. 14/13, 21/20.
[42] 9. 40, 74/75; 14. 24/29, 26/31; 43. 28/27; 48. 26.

In three other texts the term *kalima* has three different senses; in 3.64/57 an "agreement", in 18.5/4 a "statement" or "explanation", and in 23.100/102 "mere talk." The concepts are distinct but inasmuch as all three are expressions of an idea, "word" can by an allowable use of metonomy be used to indicate them.

Most of the meanings of this term, so adaptable in Arabic, go beyond what it could signify in English, even by a stretch of the imagination. In many texts it is used in the heat of poetic fervor, as a ready synonym for a more exact expression. Muslims believe the Qur'ān to be a divinely transmitted message backed by the authority of the supreme lawgiver and so not subject to the limitations of human speech. It is worthy of note, however, that the singular form, *kalima,* in accordance with its connotations explained in the first chapter, is never used in the Qur'ān in a purely physical sense of a vocal sound or a series of written letters. A divine decree, a profession of belief, an agreement or understanding, a statement or explanation and mere talk—all represent a supra-sensible operation of the intellect and will. This is not to deny that a purely sensible acceptation is possible, but actually it is not found in Qur'ānic usage.

Finally, *kalima* in its singular form occurs in three texts in a meaning that is of unique importance in this study. The first of the three occurs in 3.39/34, at the announcement made to Zechariah (father of John)[43] by an angel of the conception and birth of a son: "Zechariah prayed to his Lord and said: My Lord, grant me from thee a good offspring. Verily thou hearest prayer. And the angels cried out to him as he was standing praying in the sanctuary: God brings thee good tidings of John, to confirm a word from God". The second occurrence of the term in the same sense is in the same chapter, six verses later, 3.45/40: "When the angels said: O Mary, verily God gives thee the glad tidings of a word from him; his name is the Christ, Jesus, son of Mary, eminent in this world and the next and of those whose place is nigh to God."[44] The third and the last passage[45] in which word occurs in a like context is in 4.171/169: "O people of the Scripture! Do not go to extremes in (stating) your religion, nor say about God anything but the truth. The Christ, Jesus, the son of Mary, is only God's apostle and his word, which word (*hā*) he cast into Mary, and a spirit from him. Believe then in God and his apostles and say not Three."

---

[43] Lk 1.63. See Qur 3.38-39/33-34.

[44] 3.45/40.

[45] The expression *qawl al-ḥaqq* is used of Jesus in 19.34/35, but in a different sense—to indicate that Jesus is the "utterance of the creative command" because he was produced by God's creative word (*ḥaqq*) alone, as Zamakhsharī, *Al-Kashshāf*, explains in his comment on this verse. See *Journal of the American Oriental Society*, 91, 2 (1971), 218, and *Numen*, 20, 3 (1973), 204, note 7.

It is not the purpose of the present chapter to determine the meaning intended in the Qur'ānic verses where this special use of *kalima* occurs. It is sufficient now merely to consider some of the possible senses that an objective consideration of its context permits it to have. In the second and third instances of its use, "word" certainly refers to a person as is evident from the passages cited. In the first instance the Muslim view of the function of John the Baptist and the assent of important commentators[46] supply the certainty, that the context does not unequivocally give, that "word" is also said of a person whom John is to confirm by his testimony. Briefly then, a "word" which comes from God is called "the Christ, Jesus, son of Mary," is sent into a virgin by God himself, and is confirmed before men by the testimony of John the Baptist.

The name, "the Christ, Jesus, son of Mary", is attributed, not to the word, but to the male person indicated by word. This is clear from the masculine pronoun *hu*, "his", modifying "name" in 3.45/40; *Yā Maryamu inna llāha yubashshiruki bikalimatin minhu smuhu l-Masīḥ*. *Kalima*, being a feminine substantive, would demand a feminine modifying pronoun, *ismuhā*. But in 4.171/169 a different sense is implied. There God is said to have cast or sent into Mary, not a male person indicated by "word," but a "word" itself. The text reads *alqāhā*, "he cast it," with a feminine pronoun to supply for the feminine noun *kalima*; not *alqāhu*, "he cast him", which would indicate a masculine person sent to Mary. *Innamā l-Masīḥu ... rasūlu llāhi wakalimatuhu alqāhā ilā Maryam.*

Hence, viewing their contents objectively, from the standpoint of grammatical use and syntax, the last two texts might be freely rendered: 1. O Mary! God announces to thee a word from him. This particular male person indicated by "word" will be named the Christ, Jesus, son of Mary. 2. Jesus is not God himself but only a word of God. God sent a word to Mary in order to effect in her one of those persons who is named, after the cause of his production, a "word."

A further inquiry concerns the relationship between "word" and Jesus as they occur in 3.45/40. Is "word" to be regarded as an epithet or a kind of nickname given to Jesus, as a person might be called "Tiger" because of his tigerish disposition. Or is Jesus the name given to a "word from God," that is, to a particular class of beings who bear the title "word"? To put the matter more concretely, is there question in 3.45/40 of a certain "word" from God who is announced to Mary and who will be called Jesus at his coming or will Jesus acquire the name "word" in his lifetime?

To answer this question it will help to have at hand a verbal rendering of the text:

Yā Maryamu inna llāha yubashshiruki bikalimatin minhu
O Mary verily God announces to thee a word from him
smuhu l-Masīḥu ʿIsā bnu Maryam.
his name the Christ Jesus son of Mary.

---

[46] E.g., Ṭabarī, Bayḍāwī, and Jalālayn *in loco*.

As may be seen from the literal meaning of the passage, the Arabic, in accord with ordinary usage, does not express the verb *to be*. Hence one is left to judge from the sense of the whole and from knowledge of the persons involved whether the tense of the copula understood is past, present or future. Translators have generally rendered the passage by "his name shall be the Christ, Jesus," apparently on the analogy of the account of the Annunciation in Lk 1.31: "You will bear a son, and you shall call his name Jesus."

This rendering is in accord with the Arabic context and, if it is accepted, it would seem that "word" is here a universal term and applies to Christ as a class name or a generic title; *a* word, that is, one of those beings known as "word."[47] According to the text as it stands, then, one of a class of persons individually known as "word" is announced to Mary. When he shall come he is to be called the Christ, Jesus, son of Mary.

Exception may be taken to this interpretation of the text from the reading in 4.171/169: "Jesus, son of Mary, is only God's apostle and his word," where word is apparently definite. The objection may be answered from the text itself. Just as it is certainly not implied there that Christ is the only apostle of God—since the verse ends with an exhortation to believe in God and his apostles[48]—so it should not be understood from it that Christ is his only word. In addition, the indefinite ending of "spirit," *rūḥ* in its nunnated form, as the third name predicated of Jesus in this text, gives added probability for an indefinite meaning of all three. Finally, the omission of a relative, *allatī*, introducing the dependent clause, "He cast it (word) to Mary," is a further indication of the indefinite character of *kalima*. Thus the sentence can rightly be translated; "Jesus ... is only an apostle of God and a word of his". It is true that the Arabic could have been expressed unequivocally by the use of a longer form, for example, *rasūlun min rusuli llāh*, "an apostle from among the apostles of God," or an equivalent, but the briefer expression is preferred in eloquent style.

Inasmuch as *kalima* refers to the same person in the three texts under consideration, we can assume with the Muslim authors who have commented on these passages that it is also used there in an identical sense. But the qualification already noted must be made, namely, although "word" is used of Christ in the foregoing sense in the main clause of 4.171/169,[49] the feminine gender of the pronoun, *hā*, in the dependent clause following implies that

---

[47] I. Di Matteo, *La divinità di Cristo e la dottrina della Trinità in Maometto e nei polemisti musulmani* (Roma: Pontificio Istituto Biblico, 1938), p. 12, simply prejudges the whole question by translating this passage: "Dio ti annunzia la nascita del suo Verbo il cui nome sarà il Messia."

[48] 4.171/169; and cf. 6.34.

[49] 4.171/169 with its dependent clause reads: "Jesus ... is only God's word, which word (*hā*) he cast into Mary."

"word" is there to be taken literally. Accordingly, Jesus and other beings in the same category are named "word" because of some relation they have to word in its original meaning.

But if it bears the same meaning when applied to Jesus in these places, does "word" correspond to any of the senses of *kalima* in its various forms used elsewhere in the Qur'ān or does it appear here in an entirely new sense? In answering this question one must keep in mind that Jesus is not only a word in the texts under discussion but a word from God, that is, a divine act or expression of some kind exteriorly manifested. To determine just how the Qur'ān understands the divine operations *ad extra* is not within the scope of the present chapter. Nevertheless, from its frequent affirmation of God's omnipotence and omniscience, from the personal character of the being indicated by "word," and from the very context it is clear that the particular "word from God" that is to be named Jesus is not a written word in its literal sense nor a profession of belief nor an agreement nor an explanation nor a plea. Possible meanings, then, in this context are those of revealed message and promise, although, as will be seen presently, Qur'ānic teaching on Christ's origin and the use of a particular phrase to describe it, render them improbable. There remain, then, the meanings of God's command or decree.

Is Jesus, then, a command or a decree from God, that is, one produced by God's command or decree? If so, how is he included in that category? It is to be decided, then, whether the Qur'ān understands word in reference to Christ in one of these two senses, in an entirely new meaning, or in some one of the other Qur'ānic meanings that have here been judged unlikely or repugnant to the context.

3. Christ the Word in Muslim Exegesis

Islamic theology depends to a great extent on the extensive compilations devoted to the interpretation of the Qur'ān. This branch of religious knowledge, known as the "science of the Qur'ān and the commentaries" (*'ilmu l-Qur'āni wat-tafsīr*), together with the religious Tradition, forms the groundwork of Muslim dogmatic teaching and theological speculation. The commentaries on the sacred book of Islam generally adhere closely to the text, paraphrasing or explaining it phrase by phrase or, where necessary, word by word. The religious Tradition cited in support of the interpretations in some of the more lengthy compilations are not always reliable. Nevertheless it has a certain value, proceeding at least from the author's knowledge of how a text has been commonly accepted in popular opinion, which, in some cases, is traced back to those who lived with Muhammad himself and are believed to have heard his interpretation of the text.

The great commentaries were produced by men deeply versed in the intricate science of Arabic philology. They were in possession, too, of the Arabian legends and folklore incorporated into the Qur'ān and illustrating many of its moral and theological teachings. So their opinions are of some importance for determining the sense of any given passage. Their contribution is of less value in determining the meaning of certain technical religious terms. In this area they sometimes tend to interpret the Qur'ānic text in the light of the juristic and theological disputes of their own time without trying to discover the original meaning of the passage.[50]

Ṭabarī (d. 310/923), the most important of the commentators of the traditional school, bases his monumental work[51] of thirty volumes on the Qur'ānic exegesis of the first three centuries of the Islamic era. He was a skilful grammarian and lexicographer and was well acquainted with the theological and legal works written on the Qur'ān up to his time. Hence his work is exhaustive and has been heavily drawn upon by subsequent commentators.

On the Christological text under discussion Ṭabarī gives a rather extended commentary, although much of what he says is not of any special help in determining the meaning of the expression "word of God." From his remarks on 3.39/34 little can be gathered except that *kalima* there refers to Jesus. The "confirmation" rendered by John the Baptist consisted, according to two of the several interpretations given, in his "worshipping"[52] Jesus while both were in the womb, a notion taken from the Gospel account of Mary's visitation to Elizabeth.

The various interpretations of the text that are here listed, each with a chain of references to its source, may be summed up in a few brief quotations.

> Confirming a word from God, that is, confirming Jesus, son of Mary, and approving his laws and his conduct. ... John was the first to confirm Jesus and to testify that he was a word from God.[53] This, his confirmation of Jesus, was his worshipping him in his mother's womb. ... Some of the Bassora school skilled in the Arabic dialects have believed that the meaning of God's utterance, "confirming a word from God," is confirming a book from God, just as the Arab says: "So and so recited to me such and such a words," meaning "such and such a poem," because of his ignorance of the [real] interpretation of word.[54]

---

[50] See Arthur Jeffery, "Progress in the Study of the Qur'ān Text," *The Moslem World*, 25 (1935), 4-5.

[51] *Jāmiʿ al-bayān fī tafsīr al-qur'ān.*

[52] This worship, so called, implies no admission of Christ's divinity, as Di Matteo asserts it does, *La divinità*, pp. 7-8. The verb *sajada*, "bow down," is used in 7.11/10f and elsewhere where God commands the angels to bow down to Adam—to whom divinity is certainly not attributed.

[53] It is to be noted that the commentary retains the indefinite form of *kalima* throughout, so implying that Jesus is one of those beings called "word."

[54] Ṭabarī, *Jāmiʿ al-bayān*, 6, 372-74.

"To confirm a book from God" is, in Islamic terminology, to bear witness to the truth of a divine revelation which may have come to a previous prophet. So the Qur'ān is believed to affirm the truth of the *Injīl*, or Gospel, revealed to Jesus. But if the revelation has been received personally, the recipient witnesses to its truth by preaching what God has commanded, as Muhammad believed he was doing. This meaning of "word," however, as Ṭabarī states, is improbable, although it is commonly found in subsequent Islamic teaching.[55]

Several equivalents are proposed for *kalima* in the commentary on 3.45/40:

> The expression "of a word from him" means: 1. A message from God and an announcement from him, as one says: So and so communicated to me a word by which he gladdened me. ... 2. And some have said—to wit, Qatāda: The word which God, powerful and glorious, intended by 'a word from him' is his utterance, "Be". ... God, then, calls him (Jesus) his word because he had his origin from his word; as it is said of anything God has decreed: This is the decree of God and his immutable decision; that is, this springs from the decree of God and his immutable decision. 3. Others say: Rather, it is a name of Jesus, called so by God, just as the rest of his creation is designated by whatever names he wishes. 4. And it is related of Ibn ʿAbbās—God be pleased with him—that he said: The word is Jesus.[56]

The last contribution at first sight says little, but a careful reading shows that it excludes the first interpretation which completely detaches *kalima* from the person of Jesus. It is given on the authority of Ibn ʿAbbās (d. around 687 A.D.) a cousin of Muhammad's and one of the early Companions who as founder of Qur'ānic exegesis is believed to have recorded only the authentic interpretations of Muhammad himself. The third explanation is a gesture of despair: *Kalima* refers to Jesus; it is one of his names; but only God knows why he is so called. He gives his creatures what names he will and no one may dispute his decisions.

The second explanation holds that the creation of Jesus is not an ordinary creation. Jesus is a word from God because he owes his existence in a special manner to a word of God and to that alone. In such an explanation, Jesus is an effect named from its instrumental cause, just as something is called God's decree because it is brought about by his decree.

Yet Ṭabarī, after giving the four senses of *kalima* sanctioned by the various Traditions, returns to the first as his own preference:

> The most probable interpretation, in my opinion, is the first; namely, that the angel brought from God to Mary, as good tidings, Jesus, by God's message and

[55] See Bayḍāwī, *Anwār at-tanzīl wa-asrār at-ta'wīl*, on 3.39/34.

[56] Ṭabarī, *Jāmiʿ al-bayān*, 6, 411-12.

> his word which he commanded the angel to bring to her; the good tidings, that is, that God was creating a child from her without husband or man. And so for this reason God said: His name is the Christ, using the masculine pronoun. He did not say her name, using the feminine pronoun, even though the gender of *kalima* is feminine, because "the word" is not referred to. The name (Christ) refers to some male person but the noun "word" refers only to "good news." And so the personal pronoun referring to it (good news) is made masculine in gender, just as the personal pronouns referring to the feminine words used for offspring, beasts, and sobriquets are made masculine in gender [i.e., because of the male beings to which they refer].[57]

In such an interpretation the chief difficulty is in the gender of the pronoun modifying "name," as Ṭabarī implicitly admits by his attempt to explain it away. In short, he claims that the masculine pronoun is rightly used because "his" in the phrase "his name" does not refer back to the term *kalima*, "message," but to the male person announced in the message. There seems little doubt that the commentator was here influenced by a desire to avoid possible dogmatic conclusions at variance with his own opinion, since the interpretation he supports is as forced in Arabic as would be a similar English expression: "An announcement was just made. His name is so and so."

This preference of Ṭabarī for the sense of "message" for *kalima* is repeated in his observations on 4.171/169, "O Christians!... Do not say anything about God but the truth. The Christ, Jesus, ... is only God's messenger and his word, cast by him into Mary, and a spirit from him."[58] The sense of message for *kalima* also seems out of context here. It makes Jesus the bearer of the message and the message itself. Moreover, "he cast it into her" is an unusual way of expressing the delivery of a message. A strained poetical interpretation is even less acceptable here because the Qur'ān is making a dogmatic pronouncement which demands exactness of expression within the limits of ordinary speech.

After giving this meaning for *kalima*, Ṭabarī cites another chain of witnesses who see in the term God's creative command: "Qatāda has commented on this ... 'his word which he cast into Mary,' that is, his utterance, Be.[59] This concept of *kalima* as a creative command, then, has the support of Tradition in Islam and is favored by the other important commentators, since it appears to be based on a definite theory of creation implicit in the text.

The next great commentator, Zamakhsharī (d. 538/1144), author of the commentary, *Al-kashshāfu ʿan ḥaqāʾiqa t-tanzīl*, attaches little importance to Tradition but bases his exegesis on philological and dogmatic premises.

---

57 Ibid., 6, 412.
58 Ibid., 9, 418-19.
59 Ibid., 9, 419.

Though a follower of the Mu'tazalite school, Zamakhsharī is respected even by the orthodox and is ranked by Ibn Khaldūn far above any of the other commentators. A skilled casuist and a philologist of excellent ability, he offers interpretations that should be termed rational rather than rationalistic, striving to gloss over Qur'ānic tendencies to anthropomorphism, determinism, the intervention of the jinn in human affairs, and similar doctrines rejected by his school.

The *Kashshāf* summarizes much of the content of Ṭabarī's *Tafsīr* in explaining 3. 39/34, but on *kalima* the comment is brief and to the point. "Jesus is named a 'word' because he came into being by the word of God and that alone, to wit, his utterance, Be, without any other cause."[60] An alternative meaning is then offered. "Confirming a word from God—that is, believing in a scripture from him. Scripture is called a word just as we say the 'word' of al-Ḥuwaidarah instead of his poem." Here Zamakhsharī expresses no preference beyond his putting the meaning of creative command in first place. But his comment on the second Christological text is much clearer: 3.45/40, "Mary, God gives thee the glad tidings of a word from him. His name is the Christ, Jesus, son of Mary." In explaining this verse he renders unlikely any interpretation that considers *kalima*, not as a person, but as a message in which a person is announced: "Why is the pronoun referring to 'word' masculine [even though 'word,' *kalima*, is a feminine substantive]? Because the one of whom *kalima* is the name is a male."[61]

But the most complete and explicit reference to *kalima* as the creative command of God is to be found in his explanation of 4. 171/169:

> Jesus is referred to as God's word and a word from him because he exists by his word and his command (*amr*), nothing else, without the mediation of a father or of semen. He is called God's spirit and a spirit from him because he is the possessor of a spirit which has come into being without any part of what is endowed with a spirit, such as semen proceeding from the living father. He has been created by a creation that takes its departure solely from God and from his power alone. The meaning of 'He cast it into Mary' is: He made it reach her and produced it in her.[62]

In making the creation of Jesus independent of secondary causes Zamakhsharī expresses the common opinion of subsequent theologians. Christ is a "word" then, because "word" expresses the creative command by which he came into being.

Zamakhsharī's work is the basis for the commentary of Baiḍāwī (d. 685/1286) which is the most popular of all the exegetical studies on the Qur'ān.

---

[60] Abū l-Qāsim Maḥmūd b. 'Umar az-Zamakhsharī, *Al-kashshāf 'an ḥaqā'iq ghawāmid at-tanzīl* (4 vols.; Cairo: Muṣṭafa Muḥammad Press, 1354/1935), 1, 188.

[61] Ibid., 1, 190.

[62] Ibid., 1, 315.

Strictly orthodox in its interpretations, it was intended by its author who is considered almost a saint by the Sunnites to provide a doctrinally correct substitute for the work of Zamakhsharī and to surpass it in accuracy of grammatical interpretation and in the study of variant readings. It is one of the texts today taught in advanced schools for the study of the Qur'ān and has provided the theological basis for Muslim piety in the interpretation of its scripture.

Of the three texts in question Baiḍāwī offers a pertinent comment only on 3. 39/34:

> To confirm a word from God: that is, (to confirm) Jesus, so called because he has come into being by God's command without a father. He resembles the extraordinary things which constitute the universe of decree *'ālamu l-amr*). Or (to confirm) God's book which is called a 'word' just as one says the word of Al-Ḥuwaidarah to indicate his poem.[63]

Baiḍāwī's treatment of the question introduces a new element, the "universe of decree" or the "order of (beings created by a simple) command" of which Jesus is made a part by his special creation. He gives an indication of how this expression may be understood in his comment on 17. 85/87: "They will ask thee of the spirit (*rūḥ*). Say: The spirit is from the command (*amr*) of my Lord." Here Baiḍāwī explains that the spirit comes to be by God's command (*amr*), "Be" (*kun*), without matter, which itself is generated from something previously existing.[64] Such a solution would have the added advantage of explaining the name "spirit" (*rūḥ*) used of Jesus in 4. 171/169 in conjunction with "word" (*kalima*), "Jesus ... is only God's apostle and his word, cast by him into Mary, and a spirit from him."

A "word" then, according to such an interpretation, would indicate one of a class of beings produced by a "first creation," theologically understood, as contrasted with "second creation" or production from previously existing matter. So Christ is a word because he exists independently of secondary causes, such as a father or sperm. He is, moreover, produced from no previously existing subject, but by a special command of the Creator directly intervening. Whether or not this interpretation is altogether in accord with the intent of the Qur'ānic texts will be discussed presently.

The short but useful commentary (*Tafsīr*) of Jalālain[65] merely confirms this last opinion by its explanation of 3. 39/34: "To confirm a word, that is, a creature; from God, that is, to confirm Jesus who is God's spirit and is named 'word' because he was created by a word, Be."[66] To this interpretation along

---

[63] Bayḍāwī, *Anwār at-tanzīl*, on 3. 39/34.

[64] Ibid., on 17. 85/87.

[65] *Tafsīr al-jalālayn*, i.e., of the two Jalāls, Jalāl ad-Dīn al-Maḥallī (d. 864/1459) and his disciple, Jalāl ad-Dīn as-Suyūṭī (d. 911/1505).

[66] Ibid., on 3. 39/34.

with several others the philosopher Fakhru d-Dīni r-Rāzī (d. 606/1209) likewise subscribes in his diffuse commentary, *Mafātīḥu l-ghaib*. According to him, Christ received the name "word" as a nickname, 1. because as an infant he spoke from the cradle; 2. because he was created by means of God's word, Be (*kun*), without the help of a father; 3. because as a word makes known ideas and the truth, so Jesus guided to the truth and to the divine mysteries; 4. because he was announced in the books of the prophets so that, when he came, it was said: This one is that word; 5. because just as a person can be called "grace of God," so Jesus was called "word of God."[67] With a little ingenuity such reasons could be multiplied several times. It can be asserted with reasonable certainty that most of them are alien to the sense intended in the Qur'ān where "word" is used of Christ.

The various interpretations offered above were the starting point of a number of new senses for *kalima* developed by later speculation. In the doctrine of speech (*kalām*) as the creative activity of God, his words (*kalimāt*) became infinite in number and the causes of actually existing beings. As repetitions of the creative command, "Be" (*kun*), these *kalimāt* were conceived as the means by which the objective possibles (*al-mumkināt*) acquired existence. Muslim philosophical thought, based on Qur'ānic doctrine, considered them indeed as "words," but bearing no analogy to human speech expressed in vocal sounds. Throughout its development the *logos* theory in Islam shows the influence of notions drawn from Christian theology. There exists an undoubted parallelism between the Christian Word of God, uncreated Wisdom to whom creation is appropriated, proceeding from the Father by an operation of the divine intellect and appearing on earth incarnate in Christ, and between the Muslim *kalām*, conceived as an eternal attribute of God, a creative activity, and finally as a revelation made in time to Muhammad.[68]

The doctrine of Christ as a word from God passed from the Qur'ān into religious Tradition and thence into common use as an epithet of Jesus among Muslim writers. Thus, a Tradition having to do with the "Night Journey" of Muhammad quotes God as saying to him: "If I have created Jesus from my spirit and my word, I have written your name parallel with my own."[69] Bukhārī (d. 256/870) in his famous canonical collection of the Tradition merely repeats the words of the Qur'ān in his chapter on the prophets: "According to 'Ubādah the Prophet said: Whoever shall testify that there is no deity but God, ... (and) that Jesus is ... his word cast into Mary and a spirit from him, ... God will introduce him into Paradise no matter what his works be."[70]

---

[67] Fakhr ad-Dīn ar-Rāzī, *Mafātiḥ al-ghayb* (2nd ed.; Cairo: 1324/1906), 2, 441, as cited by Di Matteo, *La divinità*, p. 12.

[68] See *Encyclopedia of Islam*², *Kalām* and *Kalima*.

[69] Cited by E. Sayous, *Jésus-Christ d'après Mahomet* (Paris, 1880), p. 78.

[70] Bukhārī, *Al-Jāmiʿ aṣ-ṣaḥīḥ* (Cairo: 1351/1932), 2, 165.

Ghazālī, in the twelfth century, speaks of Christ as having the "spirit" and the "word": "Imitate if you will (the manner of life) of the possessor of the spirit and the word, Jesus, son of Mary."[71] An eighteenth century author cites a strange story which professes to relate an event omitted from the Gospels. While on a journey Jesus is said to have come across the skull of a person long since dead. At his prayer that it speak to him informing him of its owner, "there came to him a voice from heaven, saying: O spirit of God and his word, ask it, for it will surely inform thee."[72]

These are but a few indications of a tendency that with the mystics of Islam resulted in an indiscriminate use of *kalima* to signify first Muhammad himself and then the prophets as a class. The nebulous concept of a "word" in the Qur'ān, attached to the name of Jesus, one of the greatest prophets, the sinless miracle worker,[73] gives liberty for an almost unlimited development in the later use of the term.

This same vague use of *kalima* in the Christological texts offers, moreover, a special difficulty for the Christian theologian. In considering those passages where Jesus is so named he is disposed to read into them more than they actually contain. For the Christian Jesus is the personal Word of the eternal Father. The associating of a dogmatic fact with the term can lead one to infer an identical meaning in the Qur'ān from an apparently similar use. For a Christian, "Word" is a proper name applicable to but one Person. In the Qur'ān *kalima* is indefinite when used of Christ—a fact that illustrates more profoundly perhaps than any other Qur'ānic phrase the contrast between the two religions. For where Islam, relying on the account of its sacred book, sees merely a prophet, a sent one, a word, Christianity acknowledges the Prophet, the Sent One, the Word.

4. The Religious Situation in Arabia As a Determinant of the Qur'ānic *kalimatu llāh*.

Before asking what the Qur'ān may have intended in using *kalima*, "word," of Christ, it is necessary first to inquire what it could have intended. That is to say, in determining the sense it attached to the term it is well to consider first what *kalima* had come to mean when said of Christ in Arabia of the seventh century. This meaning in turn derives from the religious influences operative at the rise of Islam and from the conceptions already familiar to the Arabs to whom the Islamic message was first addressed. The

[71] Cited by Michael Asin y Palacios, "Logia et Agrapha," *Patrologia Orientalis*, tom. 13, 425.

[72] Ibid.

[73] 3.49/43; 5.110/109-110; and 19.19.

Qur'ān repeatedly speaks of itself as "an Arabic Qur'ān." This would imply not only that it is written in Arabic but also that it uses the cultural forms, the figures of speech, and the religious personalities and locales known to Muhammad and his fellow countrymen.[74] In particular, from what source could they have acquired the background material about Jesus which could have prepared them to hear him called a word of God in the Qur'ān?

The answers to these questions will not be found in a statistical tabulation or a detailed record of Christianity's successes and failures in the Arabian peninsula, but in an assaying of the infiltrations of Christian ideas, modified and adapted to Arab thought, that occupied the minds of those who troubled themselves about religious truths in that place and age.

Long before Muhammad would have traveled through his own country and nearby Ḥawrān and the Nabatean district as a merchant, these regions were traversed by conflicting currents of religious thought. Besides forming a natural plexus for the trade routes that linked Syria, Egypt, and Persia, they had become the refuge of sectaries and heresiarchs proscribed by the Eastern Empire. Within their borders, side by side with orthodox Christianity, heresies flourished to such an extent that the region gained the qualification "fecund in heresy" among the Christian writers of the day.

Hence the pagan Arab of Muhammad's time must not be considered destitute of religious ideas. He was in frequent contact with his countrymen who had adopted Christianity and he lived in an environment penetrated by Jewish teachings or Christian heresies,[75] especially Nestorianism whose influence was strong everywhere in Arabia.[76] In the south, Abyssinian Monophysites had established themselves and, together with the Arians, had begun to spread their doctrines in Najrān, the most solidly Christian part of the peninsula. Nor were other sects without their influence on nascent Islam. Certain teachings of Elkesaism and the sect of the Nazarenes, both similar to Essenism, bear such a close resemblance to certain points of Qur'ānic Christology that these also must be seen as part of the religious background that prepared the Arabs to receive the message Muhammad was to bring. The Qur'ān, then, speaks in a language that incorporates many of the religious ideas that prevailed in the Arabia of that time—orthodox, Nestorian, and Monophysite—all set against a backdrop of Biblical narratives and Jewish legend culled from the Talmud and Midrash.

In such circumstances it was impossible for the Qur'ān to pass over in silence the figure of Christ which, though partially obscured by heresy,

---

[74] W. Montgomery Watt, *Bell's Introduction to the Qur'ān* (Edinburgh: Edinburgh University Press, 1970), p. 185.

[75] G. Gabrieli, "Gesù Cristo nel Qorano," *Bessarione*, 9 (1901), 44, gives a list of the more important heresies flourishing at the time—some of them originating in Arabia itself.

[76] See F. Nau, "L'expansion nestorienne en Asie," *Bibliothèque de vulgarisation du Musée Guimet*, 40 (1914), pp. 211-37.

nevertheless dominated the Arabian medley of religious speculation. In the Qur'ān certain elements of Christology and, specifically, of the doctrine of the word of God, can be traced to this or that heterodox teaching. But the discordant clamor of Arabia's heresies and the thirteen centuries that have elapsed since the rise of Islam make it impossible to define these origins with exactness and to trace them to their sources.

There are not wanting, however, ecclesiastical writers who make explicit mention of the doctrines found in the Qur'ān concerning Christ the word. John of Damascus, living within a lifetime of Muhammad's death and on the scene of a still primitive Islam, relates these origins in general terms: "The false... prophet Muhammad... after consulting with a certain Arian monk, founded his own sect," and continues almost immediately with the Qur'ānic account of the Word: "For the Word of God and the Spirit, says (Muhammad), having entered into Mary, begot Jesus."[77] The Damascene's statements were afterwards amplified by authors of lesser authority and reputation, such as Bartholomew of Edessa and Euthymius Zigabenus: "From the Arians... he (Muhammad) learned that the Word and the Holy Spirit were creatures, from the Nestorians that a man, that is to say, a human person, should be adored."[78] "Muhammad, ... on a trip to Palestine, ... learned from the Arians that the word and the spirit are creatures (*ktistá*).[79]

The Qur'ānic teaching on the word of God (*kalimatu llāh*) resembles the tenets of those heretics—Ebionites, Theodosians and Sabellians—who regarded it, not as the second Person of the Trinity, but as an impersonal power or influence emanating from the Deity. But the few testimonies we possess link the conceptions of the Qur'ān in a special way to those of the Arians and Nestorians.

There is no way of determining just when Arianism began its inroads into Arabia. It is probable that its adherents in their flight from persecution introduced this heresy shortly before, but in 356 an Arian, Theophilus Indus, led to south Arabia the first Christian embassy of which there is record. Sent by the Emperor Constantius to oppose Persian encroachments, he built a church at Aden and others in the region of Ḥimyar about five hundred miles south of Mecca. Thus was established a source which joined the current of Christian ideas, sound and heretical, that circulated through pre-Islamic Arabia.

Besides the statement of John of Damascus that Muhammad's mentor was an Arian, we have the words of his disciple, Theodore Abū-Qurrah (d. about 820), one of the great Byzantine theologians: "The Agarenes... bend their efforts to one point, the denying of the divinity of the Word of God...

---

77 Sancti Joannis Damasceni, *De Haeresibus Liber*, n. 101; P.G. 94, 765.

78 Bartholomaei Edesseni, *Confutatio Muhammedis*, P.G. 104, 1450.

79 Euthymii Zigabeni, *Panoplia Dogmatica*, titulus 28; P.G. 130, 1333.

For their false prophet, since he followed the error of Arius, passed on to them this teaching, so opposed to piety and religion."[80]

As early as the beginning of the fourth century, moreover, certain Arians mentioned in a letter of the Patriarch of Alexandria were said to have held a doctrine on the divine Word that appears almost identical with that proposed in the Qur'ān:

> (The Arians affirm that) the Word of God has not always been; but that it has been made from nothing; that this so-called Son is a creature and a work; that he is not at all like to the Father in substance (*hómoios kat' ousían*) nor his true Word, nor his true Wisdom, but one of those things that has been made and created.[81]

Did the Qur'ān understand *kalima* as God's creative command? Certainly the concept was not a novelty in the Arianism whose teachings circulated in the melee of heresies that passed for Christianity in pre-Islamic Arabia. So Euthymius Zigabenus writes "against the Arians, among whom is reckoned the Samosatene (Paul of Samosata) because he too held that the Son of God is only an enunciated word and a divine command which the Father used, as a workman a tool, to create the universe," and, "The word of God is not, as a certain (Arian) may assert, orally enunciated, nor does it emit a vocal sound, nor is the Son that which God orders and commands."[82]

But if the Arians influenced the religious scene in which Islam had its rise, Nestorian doctrine seems to have been of even greater importance, given its wide diffusion throughout Arabia. But this heresy must not be conceived as teaching a unified and unchanging body of doctrine over any extended period. Its tenets varied at different times from the moderate theories which separated the two natures of Christ and denied the *theotokos* of Ephesus to the assertions of extremists who taught that Jesus was born a mere man and only later in life was granted a moral union with the Word.

Even though the majority of the Christians of the Ḥijāz and south Syria were Monophysites, yet Nestorianism in seventh century Arabia was well organized. The sect was especially strong in the north at Ḥīra where the Arab speaking population used Christian Aramaic (i.e., Syriac) as their ecclesiastical language. These Nestorian Arabs of Ḥīra were the recognized leaders of their nation and through them Nestorian influence was extended over all of Arabia.[83] Consequently the foreign element in the style and

---

[80] Theodori Abucarae, *Opuscula*, 25; P.G. 97, 1558-59.

[81] Extract from a letter of the Patriarch of Alexandria, opponent of Arius, to the Bishop of Byzantium, cited by G. Gabrieli, "Gesù Cristo nel Qorano," 45. See S. Alexandri Alexandrini, *Epistolae*, P.G. 18, 573.

[82] Euthymii Zigabeni, *Panoplia Dogmatica*, tit. 11; P.G. 130, 883D.

[83] See F. Nau, "L'expansion," 211-37; Henri Charles, *Le Christianisme des Arabes nomades sur le limes et dans le désert syromésopotamique aux alentours de*

religious terminology of the Qur'ān was dominantly Syriac and came especially through the medium of Ḥīra and the Nestorian teachers with whom the Meccans had close relationships.[84] It is not surprising therefore to find that the proper names in the Qur'ān use Nestorian forms and not Jacobite. 'Isā, the name of Jesus, and his title al-*Masīḥ* come from Nestorian Syriac[85] and Jesus himself in the Qur'ān is often referred to as a human person clothed in divinity in a way suggesting the Nestorian heresy.[86]

Ḥīra remained a Nestorian episcopal see from 510 to about 1000.[87] In Muhammad's time the Arabian peninsula was ringed by Nestorian settlements, with bishoprics at Najrān and San'ā' in the Yemen, at Socotora, at Ṣuḥār, capital of 'Umān, then known as Mazūn, at al-Khaṭṭ, in the peninsula of Qaṭar, at Bassora, Damascus, Buṣra and other centers.[88] The commercial routes of Arabia felt the zealous step of Nestorian missionaries and its desert paths carried monks and pilgrims of the sect bound for Sinai or Jerusalem.

In the midst of such activity the traces left by this heresy in the primitive soil of Islam are not difficult to explain. Such traces are found, for example, in certain beliefs expressed in the Qur'ān regarding the condition of the soul after death, which existed at that time only among the Nestorians of Persia.[89] Tradition too, relates how Muhammad heard in the market place at 'Ukāz the preaching of Quss ibn Sā'ida, probably bishop of Najrān and a Nestorian.[90] From sources of this kind Islam gained many of the ideas that led early writers to regard its preachments as a Christian heresy rather than as a religion in its own right. Like many of the early aberrations from orthodoxy, the errors of Nestorianism centered about the Person of the Son of God. Consequently, some notions of its Christology may help further to determine the influence of this heresy on the religious environment in which the Qur'ān was proclaimed.

---

l'Hégire (Paris, 1936), p. 63; De Lacy O'Leary, *Arabia before Muhammed* (London, 1927), pp. 136-37; and Michelangelo Guidi, *Storia e cultura degli Arabi fino alla morte di Maometto* (Firenze, 1951), pp. 149-50.

84 Tor Andrae, *Mohammed: The Man and His Faith* (New York: Harper & Brothers, 1955), p. 90; W. Montgomery Watt, *Muhammad at Mecca* (Oxford: The Clarendon Press, 1968), p. 27.

85 Alphonsus Mingana, "Syrian Influence on the Style of the Ḳur'ān," *Bulletin of the John Rylands Library, Manchester*, 11 (1927), 83, and J. Spencer Trimingham, *Christianity among the Arabs in Pre-Islamic Times* (London: Longman Group Ltd., 1979), p. 267.

86 Louis Gardet, *Mohammedanism* (London: Hawthorn Books, 1961), p. 38.

87 *Encyclopédie de l'Islam*,[1] "Nasara," tom. 3, 960f.

88 F. Nau, "L'expansion," p. 211ff.

89 See Tor Andrae, *Mohammed*, pp. 89-90.

90 Tor Andrae, *Mohammed*, p. 92, and J. S. Trimingham, *Christianity among the Arabs*, pp. 177-78.

One Nestorian doctrine among others that appears to have been incorporated into the sacred book of Islam is a Nestorian interpretation of the "new Adam" of Saint Paul.[91] "You (O Nestorius)" writes John Cassian, "assert the Lord Jesus to have been alike in all things and equal to Adam: Adam indeed (conceived) without seed and Jesus too without seed; the first only a man and the latter too, a man and nothing more."[92] A similar comparison occurs in the Qur'ān (3.59/52) a few verses after the second reference to Jesus as "a word from God" in 3.45/40: "Verily the likeness of Jesus with God is as the likeness of Adam. He created him from dust, then He said to him, Be, and he was." The ordinary interpretation of this verse is that Jesus was like Adam because he came into being without the aid of a father and only by the creative command of God, whence his name *kalima*, word, that is, the command to be.[93]

Even more striking is the parallelism between the teaching of Nestorius and that of the Qur'ān on the nature of the "word," if *kalima* is understood as a creative command. In his compilation of ecclesiastical history and heresiology Abū l-Barakāt, a Christian author of the early fourteenth century writing in Arabic, mentions the repugnance felt by the Nestorians toward any attributing of human experiences to a divine person. Thus they rejected the reasoning that since Christ is God, God was born, crucified, and buried. He then continues:

> It is related of them too their irritation at [hearing the Jacobites] say that the word of God was found in the womb of a woman or that the womb enclosed it. And so they comment on this explaining that the word (*kalima*) descended into her only as a command (*amr*) and she conceived (him), just as other men are conceived and in this way he (Christ) was born, a man up to the day of his baptism. ... Nestorius as patriarch of Constantinople forbade the Christians to say that the Virgin Mary brought forth God. He commanded them not to confess that he who was born of her was anything but a man like us.[94]

The similarity between the Qur'ānic Christological texts and the Nestorian doctrine here reported is all the more notable when the ideas are seen in the original Arabic where similar terminology is used. The words of the Christian author, "the word of God ... descended into Mary as a command," clarify the Qur'ānic verses that speak of Christ's origin: "God cast his word into Mary" (4.171/169); "God creates what he wishes; ... he only says to it, Be, and it is" (3.47/42).

---

[91] Rom 5.12-19, and 1 Cor 15.21f.

[92] Joannis Cassiani, *De Incarnatione Christi*, Lib. 7, cap. 6; P.L. 50, 214.

[93] E.g., Ṭabarī, *Jāmiʿ l-bayān*, 6, 467-68, on 3.59/52.

[94] Abū-l-Barakāt, *Kitābu miṣbāḥi ẓ-ẓulmati wa-īḍāḥi l-khidma*, cap. 1, *Patrologia Orientalis*, 20, 663.

The error of interpreting in a material fashion God's word by which he created all things was, however, older than Nestorius. At the end of the fourth century Theodore of Mopsuestia, on whom Nestorius, as a disciple of the Antiochean School, based much of his own teaching, asserted that the creative command of God, the *Dixit* of Genesis 1.3, was to be interpreted in a material sense as a vocal utterance intended to be heard by the angels.[95] This concept of the Biblical *eipen kai egeneto* is exactly in accord with the Qur'ānic expression of the same divine operation: "He says, *Be*, and it is (*qāla kun fayakūn*). That Theodore's teachings had lost none of their vitality in the world of religious ideas of late sixth century Arabia is attested to by their repeated condemnation[96] in the two or three decades preceding Muhammad's birth. Thus there is every likelihood that this material representation of a divine operation which is found in the Qur'ān in the verses cited and in several other passages[97] was widespread among the Christians of seventh century Arabia. As appears from Abū l-Barakāt's account, moreover, the application of such a concept to Christ, the word, produced as a direct creation in the womb of the Virgin Mary by a divine word of command without the aid of man, had already been made among the same ill-instructed and heretical sectaries. For the non-theologian it provided an easy explanation of what would be otherwise inconceivable.

Just as word had acquired the sense of creative command before the rise of Islam, so too the linking of the divine word of creation with spirit was no novelty in the Middle East when the Qur'ān combined the two in 4.171/169. The same pairing occurs in Ps 33.6, "By the word (creative command) of the Lord the heavens were made and all their host by the breath (Hebrew *rūaḥ*; Arabic *rūḥ*) of his mouth," while the Qur'ān has: "Jesus ... is only God's apostle and his word, which he cast into Mary, and a spirit from him."[98] In times still more ancient the Sumerians and Babylonians employed the two terms word and spirit in the same context to indicate a beneficent activity of their deities.[99] It is perhaps too much to suppose that remnants of the lore of

---

[95] *Dictionnaire de Théologie Catholique*, 3, 2129.

[96] I.e., (1) By the Emperor Justinian in his edict against the Three Chapters, in 544. (2) By the anathema of Pope Vigilius against sixty of Theodore's propositions in 553. (3) By the Fifth General Synod. which in 553 condemned Theodore in his person and his writings.

[97] E.g., 2.117/111; 6.73/72; 16.40/42; 19.35/36; 36.82; 40.68/70. See Rudi Paret, *Der Koran: Kommentar und Konkordanz* (Stuttgart: Kohlhammer, 1971), p. 27, on 2.117/111, and the parallel texts.

[98] In the Old Testament *dābār*, word, is often parallel with *rūaḥ*, breath, spirit (Ps 33.6; 147.18; Is 34.16; Prv 1.23; Jb 15.13; Jdt 16.14). See Louis F. Hartman, *Encyclopedic Dictionary of the Bible*, second revised edition (New York: McGraw-Hill, 1963), col. 2597.

[99] See James Hastings, *Encyclopedia of Religion and Ethics*, 12, 752, "Word."

these earlier civilizations lingered in Arabia of the early seventh century, but it is certain that the Qur'ān repeats many details found in the Old Testament, apparently acquired from oral sources. Whole sections of the Pentateuch indeed are paraphrased in several of its chapters, while explicit mention is made of the Psalms and, on one occasion, even a direct quotation is given.[100]

The two terms word and spirit conjoined were, moreover, in frequent use among the Christians of early centuries as titles for Jesus. Writings of the Fathers and ecclesiastical authors, already widespread in Muhammad's time, contain texts such as the following which might easily have found a material interpretation in the heretical environment of seventh century Mecca and Medina. Thus Tatian wrote: "That heavenly word, having been begotten a spirit of the Father and being the word from the power of the word, made the man the image of immortality,"[101] and Justin the Martyr: "That spirit and that power from God we may not conceive of as anything else but the word."[102] The phrase is especially common in Tertullian: "This spirit [Lk 1.35] of God will be the word. For as when John saith, 'The Word was made flesh,' we understand also the Spirit when the Word is mentioned, so here too, we acknowledge the Word under the name of the Spirit,"[103] and especially in reference to creation: "For ... in Isaias even then Christ, being the Word and Spirit of the Creator, had foretold of John,"[104] and "We being certain that Christ, being the spirit of the Creator, always spoke in the prophets,"[105] and "For who spoke but the spirit of the Creator which is Christ."[106]

Terms in technical use to express a doctrine tend to seep down gradually into common usage as popular bywords. This was all the more true in Muhammad's time when theological disputes had become the property of the masses. In that age political crises were frequently the result of popular religious convictions and rulers were moved to action against heresy less by ecclesiastical intervention than by the appeal of the ruled. Religious issues had an interest that moved men to declare themselves Monophysite or Monothelite much as a modern gathering might cheer a political system or a social reform.

---

[100] 21.105: "And already we have written in the Psalms after the reminder that 'the earth shall my just servants inherit,'" quoting Ps 37.29, "But the just shall inherit the land."

[101] Tatiani, *Oratio adversus Graecos*, cap. 7; P.G. 6, 820.

[102] S. Justini, *Apologia I pro Christianis*, c. 33; P.G. 6, 381.

[103] Tertulliani, *Liber adversus Praxean*, c. 26, n. 4, *Corpus Christianorum, Series Latina, Tertulliani Opera*, II (Turnholti: Typographi Brepolis, 1954), 1196. Cf. *Liber de Oratione*, cap. 1, n. 2, ibid., Pars I, 257.

[104] Tertulliani, *Adversus Marcionem IV*, c. 33, n. 9, ibid., I, 634.

[105] Tertulliani, *Adversus Marcionem III*, c. 6, n. 7, ibid., I, 515.

[106] Ibid., c. 16, n. 5, I, 529. For additional texts confer *Tertullian*, I, translated into English by C. Dodgson, *A Library of the Fathers* (Oxford, 1842), 321-24, note H.

The foregoing chapter has considered only indirect influences on the Qur'ānic use of word of God and the sense the term has when applied to Christ. The question of more proximate sources, oral and written, has been left for the following chapter. Until now the investigation has centered on a few of the more important ideas that may have determined the meaning of word of God during Muhammad's lifetime. Particular attention has been paid to the concrete sense of word of command or an order expressed in material sounds. Such an interpretation is in accord with the Qur'ānic tendency to convey theological truths through sensible images—a Biblical characteristic that has distinguished Islam through much of its history.

5. **Proximate Origins of the Qur'ānic "Word of God"**

When Muhammad first began to proclaim the passages that were later gathered into the Qur'ān, the message they contained centered on the religious ideas that were available to all who interested themselves in such matters in his surroundings. As time passed, however, more and more elements from Christianity and Judaism begin to fill out and reinforce the Qur'ānic teachings and precepts. Some knowledge of the sources of the Christian and Jewish ideas already possessed by the Arabs to whom Muhammad preached may cast light on how the Qur'ān understands these Christian and Jewish teachings. Specifically, such sources may illustrate the sense in which it understands the term *kalima* or "word" as applied to Christ.

To suppose Muhammad's knowledge of Biblical materials is not necessarily to question the sincerity of his belief that the Qur'ān was divinely revealed to him. The Qur'ān itself in 16. 103/105 refers to a teacher speaking a foreign language: "We know that they say: 'It is only a man who teaches him.' The language of him they hint at is foreign, but this (Qur'ān) is clear Arabic speech." As Torrey and Watt note in commenting on this passage, Muhammad does not deny having a human teacher but only insists that the person in question could not have helped to produce the text of what is believed to be a divine revelation.[107] Some modern Muslim scholars also hold that Muhammad was acquainted with Biblical material. They point out that, had he not known historically (as distinguished from knowledge through revelation) the materials of the Prophets' stories, he could not have understood what the Qur'ān was saying to him.[108] Assuming, then, that he

---

[107] Charles C. Torrey, *The Jewish Foundation of Islam* (New York: Jewish Institute of Religion Press, 1933), pp. 43-44, cited by Watt, *Muhammad at Mecca*, pp. 159-60. See also Watt, *Companion to the Qur'ān* (London: Allen and Unwin, 1967), p. 133.

[108] Fazlur Rahman, *Islam* (London: Weidenfeld and Nicolson, 1966), p. 16. See also the opinions of Aṣaf 'Alī Asghar Faiḍī and Muḥammad Dā'ūd Rahbar cited by J.

had some general acquaintance with Christian and Jewish religious concepts that grew as his career advanced, there arises the question of how such knowledge became available to him.

As has already been seen, Arabia of Muhammad's time and especially his native city Mecca did not live in isolation from the religious movements of that era. The many Jewish communities living in the environs of Mecca used the Old Testament in its Hebrew text or a later version. The canonical books of the New Testament too, were in the possession of the Christians in Greek, Ge'ez and Aramaic translations. Muhammad himself, in his frequent dealings with his Christian countrymen, either on commercial affairs or as a religious inquirer,[109] would have had many occasions of hearing "word" used of Christ, since the term was already one of his common appellatives among the ecclesiastical writers. Moreover, he had made a number of journeys to the Christian centers to the north, perhaps even as far as Damascus, and could easily have heard, at some liturgical function, the prologue of the Fourth Gospel with its references to the Word through which all things were created. Probably too, parts of Sacred Scripture were, in Muhammad's time, already translated into Arabic. It is more likely, however, that he and the Arabs in general heard them in improvised translations from other languages as is indicated by the many religious terms borrowed from Aramaic, Syriac and Abyssinian sources used in the Qur'ān. Snatches of parables and an occasional indirect reference show that Muhammad had some knowledge of the canonical Gospels, always referred to collectively by their Greek term *euangelion*, Arabicized into *Injīl*.

But, as is evident from the Qur'ān, the greater part of his knowledge of New Testament events must have come from apocryphal writings either directly or in some of the alterations which legends about Jesus and other Gospel characters underwent in circulating among the common people. Even though one assumes that Muhammad could read,[110] there is little chance that he had in his possession Scriptural writings of any kind. This is sufficiently clear from the Qur'ānic departures from the Old Testament, such as the return of the children of Israel into Egypt[111] and from the changes made in the chronology of the Prophets.[112] Even the Qur'ānic legends taken from apocryphal writings show some differences from the traditional texts now extant.

M. S. Baljon, *Modern Muslim Koran Interpretation—1880-1960* (Leiden, Brill, 1968), p. 68 and note; and of Aṣaf A. A. Fyzee, *A Modern Approach to Islam* (Delhi: Oxford University Press, 1981), pp. 94-95.

[109] See e.g., Euthymii Zigabeni, *Panoplia Dogmatica*, tit. 28, n. 1; P.G. 130, 1334B.

[110] See W. M. Watt, *Bell's Introduction*, pp. 33-37, and G. Gabrieli, "Gesù Cristo nel Qorano," 41.

[111] 26.57-59.

[112] 6.84-86.

Indications such as these point to oral sources, to a person or persons from whom Muhammad heard incomplete and corrupted accounts of Scriptural events, names, and titles attributed to characters both sacred and profane. This is confirmed by the lack of detail and sequence in the Qur'ānic repetitions of these stories and especially by the jibes of his enemies, who accused him of having a collaborator in the composition of the Qur'ān. "And the unbelievers say: This is nothing but a lie which he has forged and other people have helped him at it. ... Old folk's tales which he has had inscribed while they are dictated to him morning and evening."[113]

It is reasonably certain, then, that Muhammad used the services of a mentor, but the identity of the latter is much disputed among the Muslim commentators. At least for his Christological information it is unlikely that this person was Jewish. The Mishna never mentions Christ's name and the Jews of the time did not read the Gospels, so that the little information about Jesus which they did possess was confined to a few blasphemous legends[114] totally unlike the Qur'ānic accounts. A Greek or Persian Christian, probably a Nestorian, as suggested by some commentators, seems the most likely choice.

Tradition both Christian and Muslim mentions a certain heretical monk, Sergius Baḥīrā (*beḥīrā*, Aramaic for the "elect"),[115] as Muhammad's informer. John of Damascus, followed by a long series of ecclesiastical writers,[116] constantly refers to this personage, differing as to whether he was an Arian or a Nestorian and from what monastery he was expelled. The Sergius tradition is generally admitted to have some probability[117] and Sergius himself may have been a Nestorian who went beyond the tenets of his sect by directly denying the divinity of Christ. The most credible tradition indeed, makes him an Armenian monk[118] proscribed for heterodox opinions, probably Nestorian. It is known that, in the two centuries preceding the rise of Islam, the Church in Armenia, persecuted by the Persians, had also to contend with the Nestorians and Monophysites. The writings of Theodore of Mopsuestia and Diodorus of Tarsus were translated into Armenian and attempts were made to bring the clergy over to the teachings of Nestorius. Of the two heresies Monophysitism had the greater success and its gains were made permanent by the Armenian rejection of the decrees of Chalcedon toward the end of the fifth century.

---

[113] 25.4/5f.

[114] Such as the *Toledoth Jesu*. See G. Gabrieli, "Gesù Cristo," 43, notes 1 and 2.

[115] See *Encyclopedia of Islam*,[2] Baḥīrā, 1, 922-23.

[116] Nau, "L'expansion," pp. 217ff.

[117] E.g., by Sprenger, Nöldeke, Gottheil, Nau, and Maxime Rodinson, *Muhammad* (New York: Pantheon Books, 1971), pp. 47-48. See G. Gabrieli, "Gesù Cristo," p. 58, and F. Nau, "L'expansion," pp. 217ff.

[118] Nau, "L'expansion," pp. 217ff.

To identify this mentor with certainty, however, is not essential in determining Muhammad's understanding of the term under discussion. It is possible and even likely that he drew his knowledge from several of the sources mentioned by the commentators: Greek slaves of Mecca, a Christian Arab or Persian or proscribed heretics living as refugees in Arabia. Nor need we suppose that he always adopted the beliefs of his instructors. Theological abstractions and difficult points of doctrine such as the intellectual procession of the Son, though possibly known to some from whom he received the details of his teaching on Christ, may easily have been misunderstood in transmission. Certainly the real figure of Christ is dwarfed in the Qur'ān to illustrate its own specific teaching on prophetism and the prophets. In this there would have been abundant precedent in the doctrines of the Judeo-Christian sectaries—Ebionites, Elkesaites and Nazarenes—who swelled the number of heterodox opinions current in Arabia, and were part of the general environment that influenced the religious beliefs of those who heard the Qur'ān promulgated.

The tradition that associates a heretical Armenian monk with the origins of Qur'ānic Christology has special arguments to recommend it in connection with the three passages in question. In the apocryphal document entitled *Armenian Book of the Infancy* the expression "Word of God" is found in a sense and context that much resemble its use in the Qur'ān. This non-canonical work is almost certainly to be identified[119] with a Nestorian apocryphon of the same title composed in Syriac, but translated into Armenian in the last years of the sixth century, just a few decades before Muhammad began his mission of preaching monotheism at Mecca.

Here we find the stories of the conception and birth of the Virgin Mary and of her consecration to the Temple. These accounts together with the announcing of the birth of John the Baptist to Zechariah[120] all occur, briefly summarized, in the Qur'ān in the same context with the first two uses of "word" in reference to Christ. In the *Armenian Book of the Infancy* we have the same sequence, but the narrations themselves are considerably amplified. Finally, in the Armenian narrative of the Annunciation and Incarnation "word" is used three times of Jesus.

> The angel said: The Holy Spirit will come in thee and the power of the Most High will cover thee with his shadow. And God the word will take of thee a body. ..... The entry of the word of God will not violate thy womb. ..... Be it done to me according to thy saying. ... As the holy Virgin was speaking these words and humbling herself, the word of God penetrated into her by her ear.[121]

---

119 See P. Peeters, *Évangiles apocryphes* (Paris, 1914), tom. 2, xlvi-xlvii.

120 Compare *Armenian Book of the Infancy*, 2.3; 7.8; 3.1 and 3.6 and 7 with the Qur'ān, 3.35/31; 3.37/32; and 3.38/33; and 3.39/34 respectively.

121 *Armenian Book of the Infancy*, ch. 5, verses 5, 6, 8, and 9.

The Qur'ānic account of the Annunciation[122] is briefer but corresponds quite closely in content with the Armenian apocryphon.

In comparing the diffuse narration of the Armenian document with the parallel account of the Qur'ān it is noticeable that only the points that would be most likely to catch the imagination are reproduced in the latter. This fact is easily explainable if Muhammad obtained his knowledge of this apocryphal book from hearing it translated aloud, either from the Syriac or Armenian text, into his own dialect. With his vivid fancy, so often manifested in the poetical chapters of the Qur'ān, it would have been precisely these points that would have impressed themselves on his unconscious mind to be repeated later in one of the periodical presentations of a new sūra of the Qur'ān. The expression, "entering by her ear," provided just the vivid image of "word" that seems to be repeated in the Qur'ānic phrase, "He cast it (a word) into Mary." In the *Armenian Book of the Infancy* as we have it today the divinity of the word is stated, but even now not in such a way that it could not have been misunderstood by one hearing an impromptu translation. Moreover, the mentor may have glossed over or suppressed a doctrine opposed to his own personal conviction.

Another apocryphal document, the *Arabic Gospel of the Infancy*, has often been proposed as the source of some of the legends concerning Gospel characters in the Qur'ān. Until lately it was regarded as of a more recent date than the apocryphal *Gospel of Thomas* on which it was supposed to have drawn. Modern studies have shown, however, with reasonable certainty, that all the apocryphal narratives of Christ's infancy now extant[123] are traceable to one original source which itself was based partially on ancient legends, perhaps even on Buddhistic fables, and partially on fiction.[124]

But the present text existed in Arabic in Muhammad's time and its Syriac original is of an even earlier date. In this apocryphal gospel the first chapter, which is a scholion predating the rise of Islam,[125] contains the following reference to Christ as the Word: "Jesus spoke while he was in the cradle and said to Mary his mother: Verily I am Jesus, the Son of God, *the word* which thou broughtest forth as the angel Gabriel announced to thee as good tidings."[126] Comparing this text with the Qur'ānic narrative of the Annunciation, we find the miracle of Christ's talking in the cradle placed in the verse immediately following the use of the term "word of God" to designate him. "The angels said: O Mary, verily God gives thee the glad

---

[122] 3.45/40; 4.171/169.

[123] Apart from the details related in them of the Virgin Mary.

[124] See P. Peeters, *Évangiles apocryphes*, tom. 2, Introd., pp. 53-55.

[125] Ibid., tom. 2, p. 1 (text), note 1.

[126] *The Arabic Gospel of the Infancy*, ch. 1; Arabic text in Jn. Thilo, *Codex Apocryphus Novi Testamenti* (Lipsiae, 1832), p. 66. French translation in P. Peeters, *Évangiles apocryphes*, tom. 2, p. 1 (text).

tidings of a *word from him*; his name is . . . Jesus, son of Mary . . . And he shall speak to people in his cradle."[127]

The Qur'ānic text and the *Arabic Gospel of the Infancy* likewise show a close similarity in the choice of vocabulary, words with the same radicals being used throughout in both: *kallam* "speak"; *malak*, "angel"; *bashshar*, "bring good tidings"; *mahd*, "cradle." This is all the more noteworthy when the richness and variety of the Arabic language are taken into account. Equivalents for "cradle" or "crib" would have been *sarīr, midhwad* or *ma'laf* (which last is used of Jesus's resting place in the same *Arabic Gospel*, 3.1). The term used for "word" in the Arabic Gospel, however, is not the Qur'ānic *kalima*, but *kalām*, derived from the same root and sometimes used interchangeably with the former in the Arabic versions of Sacred Scripture. The difference is understandable if Muhammad heard this apocryphal account as he may have heard the Armenian narrative—that is, not in its present Arabic form but in an extemporaneous translation into the Qurayshite dialect made from the Syriac original. The manner in which "word" is used in this document would have given him no indication of its real meaning. From the text as it stands he could have concluded merely that Jesus was a "word." The meaning of the term he would have had to determine from other sources.

Besides *The Arabic Gospel of the Infancy* there is another apocryphal gospel, the so called *Protoevangelium of James*, which was in wide use among the Oriental Christians of Muhammad's time. This work was formerly considered to be a unit composed at the end of the second century. According to more recent studies,[128] however, it appears to be a combination of three different accounts, each of a different date, but all anterior to the sixth century. The section pertinent to the present topic, embodying the first sixteen chapters, is the most ancient, having been committed to writing in the last years of the second century, and entitled *The Birth of Mary, the Glorious Mother of God.* The original text reproduced in the present critical edition is in Greek, but versions were made at an early date into the important languages of the Middle East, including Coptic, Arabic, Armenian, and Ethiopic.

In this document too are found several of the events recounted in synopsized form in the Qur'ān in context with the first two uses of "word" to designate Jesus. Such are the promise of Joachim's wife to dedicate her unborn child to God (3.35/31—*Protoevangelium of James,* 4.1), the miraculous feeding of Mary in the Temple (3.37-38/32-33—*Protoevangelium*, 8.1) and the casting of lots to choose her spouse (3.44/39—*Protoevangelium*, 8.3 and 9.1). Finally, *logos* occurs in the account of the Annunciation given in the *Protoevangelium* in a use that resembles its apparent sense in the Qur'ān:

---

[127] 3.45f/40f.

[128] C. Michel and P. Peeters, *Évangiles apocryphes* (2 vols.; Paris, 1911-14), Collection Hemmer et Lejay, *Textes et documents*, vol. 1, 7-17, introd.

> And behold an angel of the Lord stood before her saying: Fear not, Mary, for thou hast found grace before the Master of all, and thou *wilt conceive by his word* (*ek logou autou*). And Mary ... replied: If I am to conceive (by a conception the origin of which is) from the Lord God the living (*apo Kuriou Theou zōntos*) shall I bring forth as every woman does?[129]

The use of *ek* and *apo* in this passage, then, indicate causality exercised on the action they modify. The concept corresponds to the common interpretation of "creative command" for "word" as used of Christ in the Qur'ān. "God creates what he wishes", says the Qur'ān (3.47/42) two verses after the announcing of "a word" from God named Jesus. "When he decrees a thing, he only says to it, *Be*, and it is." Thus the thing whose creation is decreed would come into being, as the *Protoevangelium* states it, *ek logou autou, by* God's "creative command."

From the possible sources existent in Muhammad's time we can form only a partial picture of how the ideas used in the Qur'ān originated. Much of its terminology undoubtedly came from legends passed on and diffused by oral tradition then current among the peoples of his age and environment. Many of these apocryphal accounts began to be circulated in the second century and found their way into non-canonical writings that are now lost. Others were so modified and embellished by imaginative details in the course of time that now only a surmise is possible in regard to their original content. Most of the early New Testament apocrypha were tinged with heresy[130] and their Christology shows the influence of Gnostic or Ebionite doctrines. They frequently resemble the Qur'ān in the way they understand spiritual realities. Some of the Jewish apocrypha, for example, represent God's creative command as uttered in Hebrew and depict the angels as speaking only in that tongue.[131]

From the consideration of the sources, then, both oral and written, of the Qur'ānic Christological terms it is possible to draw certain indications that favor the sense of "creative command" for *kalima* as used in verses dealing with Christ. It is highly probable that Muhammad's mentor or, at least, one of his more important mentors was a Nestorian. The sense of "creative command," as has been seen previously, was a Nestorian interpretation placed upon "word" precisely as used of Jesus. The few apocryphal New Testament works that are still extant also give grounds for this interpretation. *The Arabic Gospel of the Infancy* uses "word" of Jesus in such a way that the meaning of "creative command" is not excluded, but the *Armenian Book of the Infancy* and the *Protoevangelium of James* both suggest that meaning which appears actually to have been adopted in the Qur'ān.

---

[129] *Protoevangelium of James*, 11.2.

[130] See Stephanus Székely, *Bibliotheca apocrypha* (Freiburg, 1913), tom. 1, p. 17.

[131] Ibid., tom. 1, p. 47.

With this background in view therefore, it remains to consider indications in the Qur'ān itself that cast light on the concept corresponding to "a word" as used in the three Christological texts.

6. Muhammad's Understanding of Word of God

Several theories have been proposed in regard to Muhammad's historical understanding of word (*kalima*) when the Qur'ān used it of Christ in the three texts so far considered—3. 39/34; 3. 45/40; and 4. 171/169. One explanation says that the meaning he gave it came from hearing the term applied to Jesus by Christians in common religious usage. Its occurrence in the Qur'ān, then, would not necessarily imply any correspondance with its Christian theological meaning.[132] If, it is argued, he had suspected that the Christians were using the term to indicate a divine person, he would certainly have avoided associating it with Christ, especially in the period in which the Qur'ān strongly opposes what it represents as the dogma of the Trinity.

There are certain elements in this theory that fit in with what is known of his career. But even though it explains the meaning of "word" in the Qur'ān, it does not necessarily follow that Muhammad had no opinion of his own as to why it was used. Indeed, as has been seen, there was sufficient foundation in the various heretical misunderstandings of "word" as applied to Jesus to suggest another sense for the term—a sense that the average Arab of his time would have found easier to grasp than its profound Christian theological meaning with its Trinitarian suppositions. It is probable, then, that Muhammad did not know the meaning of "word" as Christians used it when the term was proposed in the three texts in question. But there are indications that his historical understanding of its meaning came, not merely from his having heard it used by Christians, but also because he had heard a theory proposed to explain Christ's origin.

A second theory on the use of the term *kalima* to designate Christ is proposed by Henri Lammens. It supposes the Christian origin of the term and sees in it an echo of the *Logos* of John's Prologue. But the real *Logos* of Christianity is obscured and Muhammad understood by this name only that Jesus had served as the organ and intermediary of divine revelation and the bearer of God's word to the children of Israel.[133] This "word" was the revelation sent down to Jesus in the Gospel or *Injīl* and his message to the

---

[132] G. Sacco, *Le credenze religiose di Maometto* (Rome, 1922), p. 39.

[133] See Henri Lammens, *Islam: Beliefs and Institutions* (London: Frank Cass & Co., Ltd., 1968), p. 51; and H. Lammens, "L'Islam contraffazione araba del monoteismo biblico," *Civiltà Cattolica*, fasc. 63 (1912), 12, and 3. 48/43.

Jews, as Muhammad saw it, was limited to confirming the Jewish Law and the worship of one God[134] and to foretelling the coming of another apostle, Muhammad.[135]

This meaning of *kalimatu llāh*, besides the authority of Lammens, has the support of certain lexicographers[136] who drew an analogy between the well known sobriquets, *Saifu llāh*, Sword of God, *Asadu llāh*, Lion of God, and the like, given to famous fighters on behalf of Islam, and the title *kalimatu llāh*, given to Jesus because he aided the cause of religion by his words in transmitting divine revelation to the Jews. The Tradition mentioned by Ṭabarī in commenting on Qur'ān 3. 39/34,[137] which interprets *kalima* as a "scripture" or a "divine revelation," might also be adduced in support of this opinion.

A similar explanation of *kalima* sees it as the prophetic inspiration with which Jesus was endowed.[138] For the same reason Moses, it is said, was called a word of God by the Islamic theologians.

This interpretation of word to indicate an organ of revelation has in its favor its realistic character which squares with Muhammad's historical understanding of prophetism. Yet it is scarcely distinctive of Christ since, according to Islamic belief, other prophets were equally favored by God and were likewise intermediaries of divine revelation. If it is possible therefore to discover a meaning of *kalima* that is both distinctive of Christ and in accord with Qur'ānic teaching regarding his origin, it should be preferred to both interpretations already considered.

Such a meaning is proposed by the commentators, as has been seen, in making word as used of Christ the equivalent of "creative command." In this they are seconded presumably by one of the most important theologians in Islam, Ghazālī (d. 505/1112), who assigns God's creative imperative, *kun*, "be," as the direct cause of the miraculous production of Jesus in the womb of his mother.[139] This thought is developed at some length in his exegesis of 4. 171/169, "Jesus ... is only God's ... word which He cast into Mary":

---

134 3. 50/44; 5. 117; 43. 63.

135 61. 6.

136 E.g., The author of *Ijmaʿ al-lugha* cited by L. Marracci, *Prodromus ad refutationem Al-corani* (2 vols.; Patavii, 1698), pars 3, cap. 18.

137 Ṭabarī, *Jāmiʿ al-bayān*, 6, 374.

138 See Sayous, *Jésus-Christ d'après Mahomet*, pp. 70ff. It should be remembered, however, that Islam regards its sacred book, not as inspired, but revealed—*munazzal*, "made to descend" (from heaven where the verbal original is preserved).

139 See *Sciences Religieuses*, 54 (1939), Al-Ghazālī, "Ar-radd al-jamīl li-ilāhīyati ʿIsā biṣarīḥi l-Injīl," pp. 57, 63, and 58*. More recent investigations have cast doubt on the authorship of *Ar-Radd al-Jamīl*. See, for example, Hava Lazarus-Yafeh, *Studies in Al-Ghazzali* (Jerusalem: Magnes Press, 1975).

Created beings owe their existence to causes both remote and proximate or, as is more commonly said, everything has its primary and its secondary causes. Usually an effect is attributed to its proximate or secondary cause; thus, looking at a green field, we say, "See what the rain has done," although God is really the author of the greenness. But if green plants are seen flourishing on dry ground in the heat of summer, we say, "Look at God's work," referring to the real cause, since the proximate cause is wanting. So, in the miraculous production of Jesus, the proximate cause is absent and his conception in Mary's womb is due only to the remote cause which is the "word" or creative command, *kun*, Be. True, everyone is created by this word, Be, but for Jesus there was no proximate cause since he was formed without seed, "which he cast into Mary"; that is, just as the ordinary child is formed by seed cast into the womb of his mother, so Jesus is formed by the "word" cast into Mary, namely, the order to come into being. This "word" then, is "cast" only in a metaphorical sense. In the formation of Adam too, there was wanting a secondary cause. For this reason the Qur'ān (38.75) says: "O Iblis [i.e., *diabolus*], what prevents thee from worshipping what [scl. Adam] I have created with my two hands?" But, since God has no hands, the sense is, "What I have created by my power," to indicate that Adam was not formed from seed, but by God's power, thus showing the absence of the secondary or proximate cause. The Qur'ān (3.59/52) expresses this likeness between Jesus and Adam when it says: "The likeness of Jesus with God is as the likeness of Adam. He created him [Adam] from earth, then said to him, Be, and he was.[140]

Apart from this explanation presumably offered by Ghazālī, it is pertinent to the discussion to observe the occurrences of the creative command, *kun*, Be, in the Qur'ān. It is found there only eight times[141] and always in connection with Jesus or with the final resurrection of the dead.[142] By the time of its first occurrence in the nineteenth sūra, Muhammad had announced approximately half of the one hundred and fourteen sūras or chapters of the Qur'ān. This was in the fifth or sixth year of his mission when he had had a chance to acquire more details of the various opinions current among the Christians on Christ's origin and to form his own interpretations on the matter. Three texts may be cited to exemplify this use of *kun*, Be. In relating the story of the Annunciation the Qur'ān (3.47/42) says: "She (Mary) said: Lord, how can I have a son, when man has not yet touched me? He (the angel) said: Thus God creates what he pleaseth. When he decrees a thing

---

[140] Ibid., pp. 58*-60*.

[141] The texts follow in temporal order of composition, according to Nöldeke's chronological arrangement of the sūras: 19.35/36; 36.78-82; 16.40/42; 40.68/70; 6.73/72; 2.117/111; 3.47/42, 59/52.

[142] This fact was first noticed by the commentator Muqātil ibn Sulaimān, (d. 150/767), *Tafsīr fī mutashābihi l-Qur'ān*, commenting on 36.82, cited by L. Massignon, *Al-Hallāj, martyr mystique de l'Islam* (2 vols.; Paris, 1922), vol. 2, 520 and n. 2.

(*qadā amran*), he only says to it, Be (*kun*), and it is."[143] The final resurrection is one of the doctrines most emphasized in the Qur'ān, especially in the Meccan sūras. The following two texts (36.78-82 and 40.68/70) show the Qur'ān defending this teaching against the skeptics of Muhammad's day: "Who shall quicken bones when they are rotten? Say: He will quicken them who produced them at first. ... His command (*amr*) is only, when he desires anything, to say to it, Be (*kun*), and it is." "He it is who quickens ... and when he decrees a thing (*qadā amran*), then he only says to it, Be (*kun*) and it is."

This concept of resurrection by a word was known to the Jews with whom Muhammad associated and is probably reproduced from the vivid scene in the Prophecy of Ezechiel 37: "O dry bones, hear the word (*kalima*) of the Lord. Thus says the Lord God to these bones: Behold I will cause spirit to enter you, and you shall live." Throughout the Qur'ān the resurrection of the dead is conceived of as a second creation, a re-creating which is accomplished by the creative command Be (*kun*); for example, in 17.49-50/52-53: "They (the unbelievers) say: What? when we have become bones and rubbish are we to be raised up a new creature? .... Who is to restore us? Say: He Who created you the first time."[144]

This new creation or raising up is easy for God, for when he decrees a thing (*qadā amran*), as the Qur'ānic formula states it, he merely says, Be, and it is. On the other hand Jesus, too, is regarded as one of those "decreed things" to which the creative command is uttered: "She (Mary) said: How can I have a boy when no man hath touched me? ... He (the angel) said: Thus says thy Lord: It is easy for me and we will make him a sign unto men and a mercy from us, for he (Jesus) is a thing decreed (*amran maqḍīya*)."[145] There is an evident parallelism between this passage, in which Jesus is called a "thing decreed"[146] and 3.47/42, where he is spoken of as one of those things to which, when God decrees, he merely utters his creative word, Be.

That Jesus is one of those beings brought about (like Adam) by God's creative decree is confirmed by several other Qur'ānic passages which would show that a definite theological theory of Jewish origin underlay the Qur'ānic pronouncements on how Jesus came into being. The Hebrew *ḥōq*, regulation, law, decree, used in a creation context in Jb 28.26, "He made a *decree* for the rain," would seem to explain the Qur'ānic use of the Arabic *ḥaqq* to express a similar concept. Examples would be: 19.34/35: "That is Jesus, son of Mary,

---

[143] 3.47/42.

[144] See also 21.104; 27.64/65; 34.7; and 50.15/14.

[145] 19.20f.

[146] This clause is usually regarded as impersonal, "It is a matter decreed." Grammatically, however, it is permissible to render it, "He is a thing decreed," a sense which fits more easily into the context as a third appellative of Jesus: "a sign, a mercy, a thing decreed."

the utterance of the *ḥaqq* (creative decree or command)"; 3.59/52f: "In God's sight Jesus resembles Adam. Him (Adam) he created from dust. Then he said to him, Be, and he was—the *ḥaqq* from your Lord."

This understanding of *ḥaqq* as creative decree also makes better sense of Qur'ānic passages like 6.73f/72f: "It is he who created the heavens and the earth with the *ḥaqq* (creative decree). On the day when he utters, Be, and it is, his utterance is the *ḥaqq*"; 21.16ff: "It was not in play that we created the heaven and the earth. ... Rather we hurl forth the *ḥaqq* upon the void (*naqdhifu bil-ḥaqqi ʿalā l-bāṭil*)[147] and it overcomes it"; and 34.48/47f: "Say: My Lord hurls forth the *ḥaqq*. ... The *ḥaqq* has been accomplished. Nothingness does not originate and does not restore." Translating *ḥaqq* in its ordinary sense of "truth" in these texts makes little or no sense and has always posed a problem to commentators and translators.[148]

Jesus, then, is rightly called a word, that is, a creative command or, more explicitly, a "thing decreed" by a creative command. From this it is clear that the title is applied to him in the Qur'ān by a denomination purely extrinsic; that is, merely by way of indicating the manner of his temporal origin and with no reference to anything inherent in him. "Word" expressing a divine activity hypostatized never occurred to the founder of Islam as the sense conveyed in the three Christological texts.

According to the Qur'ān Jesus comes into being merely by a special kind of divine act through which God produces creatures without secondary or proximate causes. The raising of the dead on the last day will be a second creation in which God will also produce or "restore" men directly, that is, by a simple creative command.[149] It is to be noticed that the Qur'ān further distinguishes this kind of divine act by indicating that it is usually exercised on matter already existing[150] and is, therefore, creation only in an improper

---

[147] *Qadhafa* used with the preposition *bi* means to use something as a projectile. See Rudi Paret, *Der Koran: Kommentar und Konkordanz*, p. 341 on 21.18.

[148] See *J.A.O.S.*, 91 (1971), 208-21. Ṭabarī, *Jāmiʿ al-bayān*, 11,459, in his comment on 6.73/72 gives "creative command" as one of the interpretations of *al-ḥaqq*. Zamakhsharī, *Al-Kashshāf*, 2,23, on 6.73/72 also understands *al-ḥaqq* as God's word, "Be." Recently this ancient Muslim interpretation has been defended by R. C. Zaehner, *The Comparison of Religions* (Boston: Beacon Press, 1967), p. 208. The radical *ḥqq* in Aramaic/Syriac is found in *ḥuqqā*, rule, which has a basic meaning similar to the Hebrew *ḥoq*.

[149] In 50.42/41 "On the day when they will hear the shout with the *ḥaqq*—that is, Resurrection Day," *al-ḥaqq* would seem to signify the creative command that effects the Resurrection. This command will be heard immediately after the "shout" of destruction that in Islamic eschatology brings about the death of every living creature as a prelude to the end of the world.

[150] Such a concept corresponds to the Christian doctrine of "second creation," that is, production from previously existing matter, as distinguished from "first creation," the production of a being from nothing previously existing.

sense. This is evident in the Qur'ānic account of the general resurrection and of the formation of Adam. In the former, this quasi-creative act will be exercised on bones or dust. Adam, to whom Jesus is compared in this respect, was called into being from moulded earth. "The likeness of Jesus with God is as the likeness of Adam. He created him from earth; then he said to him, Be, and he was" (3. 59/52). Presumably, he is conceived of as formed but lifeless, until the quickening word *kun*, Be, is pronounced by the Creator, just as *kun* will one day quicken lifeless bones into living beings.

How the Qur'ān regards this divine act as effecting the conception of Jesus is not explained [151] but it is apparent that it placed his production in the same category as the formation of Adam and the raising of the dead. Briefly, "a word," in Muhammad's historical understanding of the term according to the foregoing explanation, is the name given to a being created from matter already existing and independently of secondary or proximate causes. When used of Jesus it has a unique application,[152] since he alone, unlike Adam and those to be raised to life on the last day, was produced in this way in the womb of a virgin.

In the opinion of several Christian writers who have commented on the Qur'ānic use of word to indicate Christ, Muhammad, indeliberately perhaps, but implicitly, admits the divinity of Jesus. Ludovicus Marracci, writing in 1698, held that, apart from what Muhammad may have intended, the very use of *Verbum Dei* necessarily implies a divine nature in him of whom these words are predicated.[153] Others tend to believe that Muhammad accepted Christ's divinity [154] or, at least, that the Qur'ān, in employing such a term as "word of God," which has a connotation of the divine, contradicts itself in denying that divinity.[155]

In this matter, however, the theologian must dissociate the meaning of "word," as Muhammad apparently understood it of Christ, from its meaning in Christian theology. Otherwise he runs the risk of finding in the Qur'ān something that it is not meant to convey. It is true that, if "Word of God" is used of Jesus in the orthodox Christian sense as a proper name of a divine

---

[151] The sense might be that Jesus was formed of a "blood clot" uninfluenced by male seed, to express the matter in Qur'ānic terms. See 22. 5 and 96. 1-2.

[152] So Ṭabarī comments: "My [God's] creating Jesus from his mother without man was not more wonderful than my creating Adam without either man or woman." See *Jāmiʿ al-bayān*, 6, 468, on 3. 59/52.

[153] See L. Marracci, *Prodromus ad refutationem Corani*, pars tertia, cap. 18, p. 63.

[154] Ignazio Di Matteo, partially because of the Qur'ānic use of *kalima*, inclines to the opinion that Muhammad accepted the divinity of Christ. See *La divinità*, p. 13.

[155] So A. Palmieri, "Coran (sa théologie)," *Dictionnaire de Théologie Catholique*, 3, 1787: "Le terme de Verbe de Dieu suppose dans le Christ quelque chose de divin de telle sorte que le Coran, en niant sa divinité, se contradisait." Actually, the Qur'ān never denies Christ's divinity *in so many words*, as Di Matteo well shows (*La divinità*, pp. 3-13).

Person, it is not only a proof of his divinity but also an indication as to the manner of his proceeding from the Father. But such a meaning, far from being supposed in the Qur'ān, is clearly never intended.

If one is looking for such implicit but indeliberate concessions regarding Christ's divinity, investigation should turn, not to *kalimatu llāh*, but to terms and statements carried over from Christianity and retaining their original sense in the Qur'ān. Such might be the precept attributed to Christ, "Worship God, *my* Lord and *your* Lord," implying, as it does in John's Gospel,[156] that the Father is not Lord to Christ in the same way as he is to us, since Christ is divine. Or, as a modern Christian Arabic writer well shows, the statement in the Qur'ān (5.110) that Christ created a bird, breathing life into it, is an implicit admission that he is God, since no creature can possess or exercise such a power.[157]

Christian controversialists[158] have objected to the interpretation of word as a creative command, here upheld, on the grounds that it does not signify anything proper to Christ alone. For this reason the interpretation of creative command has not been investigated by Western writers. To say that Christ is called a word, they argue, because he was created by a word or creative command is simply to class him with all creatures, since the Creator "spoke, and it came to be, he commanded and it stood forth."[159] But, as has been already explained, Islam defines the peculiar kind of creation accomplished by a divine command, Be, to which it attributes Christ's origin, as a production independent of proximate causes and so distinguishes it from the ordinary creation, so called, in which the Creator employs the mediation of creatures.

A further objection claims that such an appellation is forced, just as if one should call "water" a person cleansed by water or "fire" one warmed by fire. But the answer to this is that, even though word as used of Jesus in the Qur'ān is a class name, yet his inclusion in that class is unique, since only he was produced in his mother by God's creative command alone. A prophet as highly endowed as the Qur'ān conceives Jesus to be is deserving of a distinctive title. Moreover, even before the three Christological texts of the Qur'ān had

---

[156] Jn 20.17 and Qur'ān 5.117. See *Zeitschrift der Deutschen Morgenländischen Gesellschaft*, 131 (1981), 273-80.

[157] P. Sbath, *Al-Mashra'* (Ar-Ri'ah Press, n.d.), p. 91. Jn 1.3 and Heb 1.2 attribute creative power to Christ as a proof of divinity and theologians commonly deny to creatures even an instrumental causality in that divine activity. It is true that there is question in 5.110 only of second creation, but the concept of first creation seems not to be found in the Qur'ān. See *Z.D.M.G.*, 120 (1970), 274-80.

[158] E.g., L. Marracci, *Prodromus*, pars tertia, cap. 18, pp. 61-63, and Sbath, *Al-Mashra'*, pp. 89-90. See also Bartholomaei Edesseni *Confutatio Agareni*, P.G. 104, 1398D; and Demetrii Cydonii, *Contra Mahometem*, P.G. 104, 1130f.

[159] Ps 33.9.

been promulgated, Muhammad had heard from his instructors both the term and probably too the explanation of it which he accepted. Consequently, those who taught him and not he, are to be blamed for any discrepancy in terminology. Finally, mere examples, such as the use of "fire" or "water" prove little, since similar examples can be adduced to prove the contrary. The commentators cite a parallel in the common Arabic expression, "That event is God's decree," because it was caused by his decree. Or, to use English comparisons, a shoot or twig is called a "graft" because it is inserted by a graft and a meal of sea food is called a "bake" because it is cooked by a bake. Moreover, it is to be noted that word, in its apparent meaning in the Qur'ān as used of Christ, is not said indiscriminately of all creatures, but only of rational beings. It is expressly applied only to Christ, and the type of divine activity it implies is exercised only on him, on Adam, and on those to be raised from the dead on the last day.

But difficulties of this kind, presented by Christian critics, are best explained by recalling two points that have already been stressed in the course of this study. First, the question here treated is *de facto* and not *de jure*. The discussion is on the Qur'ān's actual understanding of the term word, not on what it should have understood by it. Second, one must deny the supposition that underlies such objections; namely that word is intended in the Qur'ān to distinguish Christ from every other being. On the contrary, "word," as used of Jesus there, is indefinite, "*a* word." So, as already noted, it merely places him in a certain class of beings—for a unique reason, it is true—but is not intended as a name proper to him alone. Word or *Verbum* as a proper name is a Christian idea, not Muhammad's idea. Therefore to see in it only the sense it has in Christian theology is to prejudice the entire investigation of its meaning as known historically by Muhammad and as used in the Qur'ānic message which he regarded as divinely revealed.

7. Islamic Speculation and Christian Polemics on *kalimatu llāh*

As might be suspected from its uncertain meaning, *kalima* and its cognate *kalām* gave rise in Islam to a long series of speculations. A brief review of their development will be of help at this point to understand the objections of Christian controversialists. One of the earliest applications of *kalima* in the primitive Muslim community was to the Qur'ān. Muhammad had proclaimed it as a scripture containing the very words of God but the piety of his followers went even farther, making it uncreated and coeternal with the Deity. Under Christian influence Islam evolved the concept of an eternal "word," corresponding to the divine Word in the Christian doctrine of the Trinity, but made tangible in the book sent down by God to Muhammad. Finally the orthodox theologians of Islam applied the notion to the Qur'ān in its actual linguistic form.

After futile objections by the liberal Muʿtazilite school this opinion was imposed under al-Mutawakkil (d. 247/861) and definitely became the orthodox belief when the famous Islamic doctor, al-Ashʿarī (d. 324/936), had publicly maintained that the Qur'ān, written or recited, was identical with the eternal and uncreated word of God. Some idea of what followed from such a doctrine can be had from one example—the official teaching that made "word" a synonym of the divine essence.[160]

Later theologians attempted to modify this doctrine by making "word" a divine attribute, subsisting in God, as do his knowledge and power, as a "simple idea." The linguistic expressions of the divine word may vary but it itself remains one and unchanging, pronounced by God without tongue or articulate sound. This word may be a prohibition, a command or a logical predication. Thus God creates only by the command, "Be" (*kun*), which is itself uncreated. In this last sense "word" is the manifestation of the divine attribute of creative power (*takwīn*) which in turn, is conceived as causing life (*iḥyā'*), conserving beings in existence (*razq*) and, in accord with the orthodox teaching that regards death as a positive entity, productive of death (*imāta*).[161]

Nevertheless, the authors of such speculation hold that Jesus, despite his Qur'ānic title *kalima*, is created, since he is God's word only in a figurative sense and by an extrinsic denomination that does not affect his nature. But Christian apologists ignored or disregarded this distinction to seize upon the apparent admissions by Islam of a Christian dogma. John of Damascus writes:

> Ye (Saracens) say that Christ is God's word and his spirit. Word ... and Spirit cannot be separated from him in whom they are naturally found. If, therefore, he (Christ) is in God as his word, he is evidently also God. But if he is outside of God, it follows from your belief that God is without word and spirit. Thus do ye mutilate God.[162]

John's argument is unanswerable, if "word" is understood of God in its Christian sense. But as it stands it is but another testimony to the traditional Christian belief, since no Muslim who knew the Qur'ān and its commentators would grant such a meaning.

The same objection is proposed in another form in treating of the divine command that effected created beings. In this matter the Christian, who speaks in an apologetic dialogue assigned to the Damascene, assumes that the Islamic teaching and his own are identical, at least on this point. "Before all ages God's word ... created all things as my Scripture and yours (the Qur'ān)

---

[160] Massignon, *Al-Hallāj*, 2, 654ff.

[161] *Encyclopédie de l'Islam*[1], 1, 312 "Allah."

[162] *De Haeresibus Liber*, 101, P.G. 94, 768C.

both testify."[163] But the Qur'ānic teaching on the creative command "Be," *kun*, simply stops at the word itself. The creative command that Islam admits is an audible voice that sends forth its vibrations as does any sensible sound or, at most, it is a figurative expression for divine omnipotence. In Muslim belief there is no trace of a divine hypostasis to whom is appropriated the activity that terminates in a finite universe.

John's disciple, Theodore Abū-Qurrah (d. about 820) refutes the Muslim attempt to prove that Christ the Word is a creature by the Muslim comparison of Jesus with the words of God in Scripture, admitted by the Christian to be created.[164] The difficulty is treated as a verbal one and is disposed of by a distinction made between God's Scriptural revelation in the Old and New Testaments (*rhemata*) and the technical term *logos* used of Christ.[165] The same distinction had previously been drawn in the dialogue attributed to John himself.[166] It illustrates the difficulty the theologians of that age found in handling a question proposed in terminology apparently identical but in reality wholly foreign in meaning to their own. Insistence on the traditional term and a clear defining of its real sense was the best answer at the time, since Islam was in the position of a newcomer who sought to cast the discussion in terms to which he had attached a new and wholly different meaning.

Both John of Damascus and his disciple lived among those who professed the beliefs which they both rejected. They could read and cite Muslim beliefs in the language in which they were proposed. Many subsequent condemnations, however, came from the pens of writers with only a slight knowledge of Islam, and that gathered from hearsay and secondary sources. Many of their rejections of Muslim tenets took the form of tirades against Muhammad and Muslims in general. Most often their own superior culture bred a disdain for what they regarded as anthropomorphisms in the Qur'ān that prevented them from undertaking any exact study of its theology.

Nevertheless, in addition to these many, there were some, especially after the first centuries of Islam, who were well acquainted with the doctrines they opposed. Even they, however, approach the dispute less with the intention of discovering the real belief of the adversary and proceeding from there than of directly expounding their own beliefs. Among these latter, Bartholomew, a monk of Edessa, attacks Muhammad's teaching in a dialogue carried on

---

[163] S. Joannis Damasceni, *Disputatio Christiani et Saraceni*, 4; P.G. 94, 1589-90.

[164] See Richard Bell, *The Origin of Islam in Its Christian Environment* (London: Frank Cass & Co., Ltd., 1968), p. 210.

[165] Theodori Abucari *Opuscula*, 36; P.G. 97, 1592. More modern studies by Georg Graf show that many of these disputations with Muslims have been falsely referred to Theodore. See *Lexicon für Theologie und Kirche*, 1, "Abū Kurra."

[166] *Disputatio Christiani et Saraceni*, 2; P.G. 94, 1587A-B.

between himself and an imaginary Muslim adversary. His polemic, though based on fairly accurate information, is characterized by lavish abuse, biting irony, and the frequent introduction of statements and concepts most offensive to a Muslim. By what right, he asks, do you give the name word of God to your volume, so often trampled under foot? If your book is cast into a well where it cannot help or free itself, how can you dignify it by that title?[167] Or again, O fool, if to Christ we are to compare Adam because he too was made without seed, it would follow by your reasoning that the first ass, dog and serpent, also formed without seed, could be put on a par with them both.[168]

A much less impassioned approach is adopted by Nicetas of Byzantium who has left one of the best specimens of Byzantine controversy against the Qur'ān. Basing his appeal on reason, he presents the following argumentation against the Islamic understanding of word of God. Things with different natures are substantially different and have substantially different properties. God, angels, and men differ, therefore, in substance and in their faculty of intellection. This essential difference in intellect is based not only on the distinction between Creator and creature, immaterial and material, but also on the "word" proper to each. In creatures "word" is not identified with their substance, but in God it is both substantial and inherent, inseparable too, from him from whom it proceeds. Wrongly, then, did the untutored Muhammad believe that things substantially different have the same natural properties and that God's self-subsisting Word is like the perishable word of mortal men.[169]

Another important polemic against the Qur'ān was composed by the Emperor John Cantacuzene. After stating that Muhammad held Nestorius's opinion of Christ, making him a mere man, although superior to all others, he inquires why he called Jesus by the title "word of God." Is it because Christ announced the word of God to men? But since the prophets did the same, why should Christ alone be called for that reason a "word"? Or is the name a way of indicating that the archangel Gabriel announced to the Virgin Mary the tidings of his coming? If so, why is the same title not given to Samson, son of Manoah,[170] and to John, son of Zechariah, both announced by an angel and born of God's promise? Hence, he concludes, it is not for these reasons that Muhammad called Christ a "word," but rather because he had heard the title from the Scriptures and used it without knowing its meaning.[171]

Other controversialists of less importance used similar arguments. Some simply repeat the accusations of their predecessors, taking "word" in the

---

[167] Bartholomaei Edesseni *Confutatio Agareni*; P.G. 104, 1410C.
[168] Ibid., 1398D.
[169] Nicetae Byzantini *Refutatio Mohamedis*, Contradictio 19; P.G. 105, 778-79.
[170] Jgs 13.3-24.
[171] Joannis Cantacuzeni *Contra Mahometem Oratio*, 3, 3; P.G. 154, 651 and 654.

orthodox Christian sense as the second Person of the Trinity,[172] just as the Muslims on their side used it in their own sense, as an effect named from the creative command that produced it. Arguing on the same basis, the Muslim admission that God is a being both uncreated and intelligent was sometimes used to show that his intellectual activity or "word" must also be uncreated.[173]

The theologians of the West in attacking the Qur'ān were even more abusive and ill-informed than those of Byzantium. But among the Franciscan and Domincan controversial writers were developed competent scholars who were the first Western theologians to investigate Arabic sources and to initiate a methodical Christian apologetic against the Muslims. To one of the latter, Ricoldo da Montecroce, is owed one of the most careful studies of the Qur'ānic use of the name "word of God" from a Christian point of view.

"Word of God" in the Qur'ān, he reasons, must indicate a personal word and not merely something accidental to Christ, because to call Christ a word only because he announced God's word would leave him on a plane with other prophets who did the same. Therefore, the Qur'ān must mean that Christ is the Word which proceeds from God eternally and through which all things were made. But whatever proceeds from God is essentially God and every word is distinct from the one pronouncing it. Since, however, no distinction is admissible in God's essence, his word must be personal. Here then, we have the Word by which God said, "Let them become, and things were made," and of which Saint John in his Prologue affirms, "All things were made through him." But every word is intellectually begotten by the one uttering it and so the Word of God is God's Son. God in his infinite perfection and simplicity, however, cannot beget another nature or a second God. Therefore Muhammad, had he been able to understand the real consequences of his assertions in the Qur'ān, would have been forced to admit that Jesus, as the Son of Mary, is man and, as Word of God, God.

But in the Qur'ān Muhammad compares Jesus to Adam whom God created from slime of the earth and to whom he said, "Be." How then, does this fit in with the preceding statements? After rejecting other interpretations, Ricoldo concludes: God said, "Be," to Adam by his Word, the very Word by which he made all things and which existed from eternity with God, that is, Christ, himself true God.[174]

Ricoldo admits that Muhammad never drew the conclusions which he himself draws from the Qur'ānic use of *kalima*. But he mentions the sense of

---

[172] Nicetae Choniatae *Thesauri Lib*. 20. 4; P.G. 140, 110.

[173] Euthymii Zigabeni *Dialogus Christiani cum Ismaelita*; P.G. 131, 38-39.

[174] Demetrii Cydonii *Contra Mahometem*, 15, qq. 2 and 3; P.G. 154, 1130-34. This is the fourteenth century translation into Greek of Ricoldo's original Latin treatise against Islam.

"creative command" which is seemingly the real understanding of the term in the three Christological texts, only to identify it with Christ. But the passages where it occurs leave the term indefinite and applied to Jesus by extrinsic denomination referring to a mode of activity exercised on him by the Creator. So Ricoldo's discussion merely uses the Qur'ānic term as a starting point for an exposition of Christian doctrine. There is no attempt made to clarify its real meaning in the original text.

Polemical writers of medieval times seem to have regarded the Qur'ān as a reasoned theological document instead of a religious and moral message, phrased in poetical cadences, whose purpose was to rouse and grip the hearts of those who heard it. Perhaps their view of the subject came from reading into the Qur'ān the speculations that rose among scholastic thinkers in Islam after several centuries of doctrinal development based on Hellenistic philosophy and science. At any rate its primary result was to further the progress of Christian theology rather than to convince Muslims that the Qur'ān was inconsistent in calling Jesus a "word" and at the same time denying his divinity.

* * *

The vast majority of Christian controversialists seem never to have met Islam on its own ground. In that era there was rarely, if ever, any agreement on the subject of the debate. The source of the difficulty probably lay in the temperament of the age when people tended to attribute culpable ignorance or bad faith to anyone who disagreed with them in religious matters. In fact, however, both Islam and Christianity hold many basic doctrines in common and in today's secularistic world both are more willing to see good and to respect sincerity in any creed that accepts moral and spiritual values. The change in attitude was not to come about until mankind had grown to greater maturity. Many centuries were to pass before an ecumenical council would say: "The plan of salvation also includes those who acknowledge the creator. In the first place among these are the Muslims. ... Upon the Muslims, too, the Church looks with esteem."[175]

---

[175] Vatican Council II, *Dogmatic Constitution on the Church*, n. 16; *Declaration on Non-Christian Religions*, n. 3.

Bibliography

Allard, Michel, May Elzière, and others. *Analyse conceptuelle du Coran sur cartes perforées.* 2 vols. and a file of 431 cards. Paris: Mouton, 1963.

Andrae, Tor. *Mohammed: The Man and His Faith.* Translated by Theophil Menzel. Harper Torchbooks. New York: Harper & Brothers, 1955.

Augustine, Bishop of Hippo. *The Literal Meaning of Genesis.* Translated by John Hammond Taylor. New York: Newman Press, 1982.

Baljon, J. M. S. *Modern Muslim Koran Interpretation—1880-1960.* Leiden: Brill, 1968.

Al-Bayḍāwī, ʿAbd Allāh b. ʿUmar. *Anwār at-tanzīl wa-asrār at-tawīl.* Jidda: Asad Muḥammad Saʿīd al-Ḥabāl and Sons, n.d.

Bell, Richard. *The Origin of Islam in Its Christian Environment.* London: Cass, 1968.

———. *The Qur'ān Translated, with a Critical Re-arrangement of the Surahs.* 2 vols. Edinburgh: T. & T. Clark, 1960.

Blachère, Régis. *Le Coran.* Paris: Maisonneuve, 1949-1950.

———. *Le problème de Mahomet.* Paris: P.U.F., 1952.

Caetani, Leone. *Annali dell'Islam.* 10 vols. Milan: Hoepli, 1905-1926.

Charles, Henri. *Le Christianisme des Arabes nomades sur le limes et dans le désert syro-mésopotamique aux alentours de l'Hégire.* Paris, 1936.

Di Matteo, Ignazio. *La divinità di Cristo e la dottrina della Trinità in Maometto e nei polemisti musulmani.* Biblica et Orientalia, 8. Roma: Pontificio Istituto Biblico, 1938.

Flügel, Gustavus. *Concordantiae Corani Arabicae.* Leipzig: Tauchnitii, 1842; reprint: Ridgewood: Gregg Press, 1965.

———. *Corani textus arabicus.* Leipzig: Sumptibus Caroli Tauchnitii, 1883; reprint: Ridgewood: Gregg Press, 1965.

Fyzee, Asaf A. A. *A Modern Approach to Islam.* Delhi: Oxford University Press, 1981.

Gätje, Helmut. *The Qur'ān and Its Exegesis: Selected Texts with Classical and Modern Muslim Interpretations.* Translated and edited by Alford T. Welch. London: Routledge & Kegan Paul, 1971.

Al-Ghazālī, Abū Ḥāmid b. Muḥammad. *Ar-radd al-jamīl li-ilāhīyati ʿIsā biṣarīḥi al-Injīl.* Critical text with translation and commentary by Robert Chidiac. Paris: Bibliothèque de l'Ecole des Hautes Études, Sciences Religieuses, 1939.

Graf, Georg. *Geschichte der christlichen arabischen Literatur.* 4 vols. Città del Vaticano: Bibl. Apost. Vat., 1944-1951.

Guidi, Michelangelo. *Storia e cultura degli Arabi fino alla morte di Maometto.* Firenze, 1951.

Henninger, Josef. *Spuren christlicher Glaubenswahrheiten im Koran.* Schöneck: Neue Zeitschrift für Missionswissenschaft, 1951.

Ibn Hishām, ʿAbd al-Mālik. *The Life of Muḥammad.* Translated by Alfred Guillaume. London: Oxford University Press, 1955.

Jalāl ad-Dīn al-Maḥallī and Jalāl ad-Dīn as-Suyūṭī. *Tafsīr al-Jalālayn.* Cairo: ʿAbd al-Ḥamīd Aḥmad Hanafī, n.d.

Lammens, Henri. *Islam: Beliefs and Institutions*. London: Frank Cass & Co., Ltd., 1968.
Lebreton, Jules. *Les origines du dogme de la Trinité*. 6th edition. Paris: Beauchesne, 1927.
Marracci, Ludovicus. *Prodromus ad refutationem Al-corani; Refutatio Alcorani*. 2 vols. Patavii 1698.
Massignon, Louis. *Al-Hallāj, martyr mystique de l'Islam*. 2 vols. Paris, 1922.
Michel, C., and P. Peeters. *Évangiles apocryphes*. 2 vols. Paris, 1911-1914. Collection Hemmer et Lejay, *Textes et documents*.
Nöldeke, Theodor. *Geschichte des Qorans*. 2nd edition, by Friedrich Schwally, G. Bergstrasser, and O. Pretzl. 3 vols. Leipzig: Dieterich'sche Verlagsbuchhandlung, 1909-1938. Hildescheim and New York: Georg Olms Verlag, 1970.
O'Leary, E. de Lacy. *Arabia before Mohammed*. London: Kegan Paul, Trench, Trübner, 1927.
Pareja, Felix M. *Islamologie*. Beyrouth: Imprimerie Catholique, 1957-1963.
Paret, Rudi. *Der Koran: Kommentar und Konkordanz*. Stuttgart: W. Kohlhammer Verlag, 1971.
———. *Der Koran: Übersetzung*. Stuttgart: W. Kohlhammer Verlag, 1962.
Parrinder, Geoffrey. *Jesus in the Qur'ān*. London: Faber and Faber, 1965.
Peeters, P. *Évangiles apocryphes*. 2 vols. Paris, 1914.
al-Qur'ān. Cairo: Al-Amīriyya Press, 1344/1925.
Rahman, Fazlur. *Islam*. London: Weidenfeld and Nicolson, 1966.
Rodinson, Maxime. *Muḥammad*. Translated by Anne Carter. New York: Random House, 1980.
Roest Crollius, Ary A. *The Word in the Experience of Revelation in Qur'ān and Hindu Scripture*. Rome: Università Gregoriana Editrice, 1974.
Sacco, Giuseppe. *Le credenze religiose di Maometto*. Rome, 1922.
Sayous, Edouard. *Jésus-Christ d'après Mahomet*. Paris-Leipzig, 1880.
Sbath, P. *Al-Mashraʿ*. Ar-Rīah Press, n.d.
Székely, Stephanus. *Bibliotheca apocrypha*. Freiburg, 1913.
aṭ-Ṭabarī, Abū Jaʿfar Muḥammad ibn Jarīr. *Jāmiʿ al-bayān fī tafsīr al-qur'ān*. Edited by Maḥmūd Muḥammad Shākir. 16 vols. incomplete. Cairo: Dār al-Maʿārif, 1957-1968.
Thilo, Joannis C. *Codex apocryphus Novi Testamenti*. Lipsiae, 1832.
Torrey, Charles C. *The Jewish Foundation of Islam*. New York: Jewish Institute of Religion Press, 1933.
Trimingham, J. Spencer. *Christianity among the Arabs in Pre-Islamic Times*. London: Longman Group Limited, 1979.
Watt, W. Montgomery. *Bell's Introduction to the Qur'ān*. Edinburgh: Edinburgh University Press, 1970.
———. *Companion to the Qur'ān*. London: Allen and Unwin, 1967.
———. *Muhammad at Mecca*. Oxford: The Clarendon Press, 1968.
———. *Muhammad at Medina*. Oxford: The Clarendon Press, 1966.
az-Zamakhsharī, Abū l-Qāsim Maḥmūd b. ʿUmar. *Al-Kashshāf ʿan ḥaqā'iq ghawāmid at-tanzīl*. 4 vols. Cairo: Muṣṭafa Muḥammad Press, 1354/1935.

General Index

(The Arabic article *al-*, with its variants, *at-*, *ath-*, *ad-*, etc., is disregarded in the alphabetical listing.)

Index to Qur'ānic References

(Numbering of Verses: Cairo/Flügel)

Index of Biblical Passages

c)